Breaking

the

Fourth Wall

An Uncertain Journey
on Turkey's Lycian Way

Michelle Sevigny

MONTLUCE PUBLISHING

Gabriola ○ British Columbia ○ Canada

Breaking the Fourth Wall: An Uncertain Journey on Turkey's Lycian Way

Published by MontLuce Publishing, 2016
Gabriola, British Columbia, Canada

Original cover design by Robb North
Modified cover design by MontLuce Publishing and
CoverDesignStudio.com
Interior design by MontLuce Publishing
Editing by Kathy Garland

Library and Archives Canada Cataloguing in Publication

Sevigny, Michelle, 1969-, author
       Breaking the fourth wall: an uncertain journey on
Turkey's Lycian Way / Michelle Sevigny.

Issued in print and electronic formats.
ISBN 978-0-9881175-3-2 (softcover). --ISBN 978-0-9881175-4-9 (ebook).

       1. Sevigny, Michelle, 1969- --Travel--Turkey--Lycia.
2. Hiking--Turkey--Lycia. 3. Lycia--Description and travel.
4. Turkey--Description and travel. I. Title.

DR429.4.S48 2016   915.6104'12   C2016-907874-4
                                           C2017-900148-5

AUTHOR'S NOTE

This book was written using a combination of memories, trail notes, photographs and conversations with people I met along The Lycian Way. While all stories in the book are true, some names and identifying details have been changed to protect the privacy of individuals who could not be contacted for permission. Finally, conversations throughout the book have been recalled to the best of my ability, and while not verbatim, the essence is accurate.

For Dad,

Respond to every call that excites your spirit.

—Rumi

DAY 0

Arriving in Ovacik

TWO BANGS ON THE DOLMUŞ signal the driver to brake, horns rebel. My stretch to the side door frees my bulging backpack to pick a fight with one passenger and high-five another. After fiddling too long with the handle, I yank open the sliding door and city noise surges in. But my senses narrow onto the teenage girl in a head scarf who holds out a small flat item with a broken, dangling strap. Hiking poles flail like first-time chop sticks as I slap my left hip, right hip. Really? Mine? How? With no idea how to pronounce the 14-letter thank you, I clap my palms together and bow. Somebody slams the door as I reunite with my over-the-shoulder, wallet-purse in a two-handed squeeze—cell phone, cash, bank card, credit card, passport and all the emergency photocopies. Impostor syndrome explodes and my eyes hide as we bounce along, like a dozen eggs in a shopping cart driven by an eight-year-old boy.

Why am I here?

I have no fucking idea.

Wait, that's not true.

Fifteen months ago, my ten-year-old Rottweiler, heart-dog and business partner, died of bone cancer. Eight months ago, I stood for the first time at a Mexican intersection where my mom had been killed in a cycling accident seven years earlier. The next day my apartment sold back home. And the day after that, my dad's wife was diagnosed with brain cancer. Six days later, we drove across the Mexico-USA border, and I flew into Victoria, British Columbia, Canada, just hours before she died. Decluttering had already started, but during the next month, I sold or donated almost all of the rest of my possessions. Leaving two free patio chairs on the front lawn, I boarded a two-hour ferry and settled into a basement suite ten minutes from my dad's house.

Then I wanted everything to stop.

I wanted to catch up. I wanted to sprawl on the forest floor for maximum grounding. But a tiny part of me needed something else. And as I ran solo along Willow's Beach at sunrise, I heard it: *Do more of this.* More of what?

"Want to hike the Rockies?" my hiker friends had asked over the years.

"Nah, I don't like hiking."

"Want to hike the Peruvian highlands?" asked others.

"Nah, I don't like hiking."

"Want to hike the West Coast Trail?" asked my sister a few years ago.

"Nah. Wait, coast?"

Within hours on the trail, I realized it wasn't hiking that I didn't like, it was hiking inland. I always chose coastal countries when travelling and adored the freedom of independent road trips and the slow speed of cycle-travel. But long-distance coastal hiking demanded a deeper simplicity and reimbursed with greater self-awareness. I was hooked.

I searched for them—the Camino de Santiago del Norte, the California Coastal Trail, the Wales Coast Path and the Lycian Way.

Maybe it was the photo my dad took of my then-29-year-old mom in front of a Turkish mosque during a three-month European road trip while I waited at home for the letters. Maybe it was the Turkish Tourism Board map dotted with red triangles for camping—requested and received by mail, 15 years ago.

I invited friends, my sister, but no one could come. I don't even know why I asked. I knew this was meant to be a solo adventure. Was it for a final healing or for something I wouldn't fully understand until it was over? Either way I needed to do it. Otherwise, I'd procrastinate from work, reading about people who'd done it. I'd drink too much to fill a void that could only be filled by hiking it. And my next dog would not find me until I'd done the thing that needed to be done without a dog.

But I still created reasons why not:

You don't have the money.

Your business needs you.

You haven't exercised in months.

And who do you think you are to go on such a journey?

But with the sale of my apartment, I had the money. With self-employment, I had the time. And with seven months, I could get physically fit again.

But why was I still hesitant?

I'd solo travelled before—cycled the Greek Islands, bussed through Ecuador and motorcycled across Northern Ireland.

Why did this feel so different?

Wild camping. Alone.

Navigating. Alone.

Losing my way in the Turkish mountains. Alone.

Then seven months later, a snapshot moment in the Istanbul airport bathroom had reminded my jetlagged brain that I was 9000 kilometres from home. A woman on my left in a pink head scarf, jeans and high heels spoke Turkish to the woman on my right, who was dressed in all black, head scarf, long-sleeves and floor-length skirt. I stared straight ahead at the sign above the triple sinks—a drawing of a foot in a red circle, slashed by a red line. No feet in sinks. What were those cleansing rituals again about washing body parts before prayer time? I regretted not studying more about Muslim customs instead of worrying about maps and solar batteries.

I follow two people off the bus and they point up the street to the Green Peace Hotel. After 27 hours of flying and layovers, an overnight stay in Antalya, and four-and-a-half hours of bus travel, I'm here in Ovacik. Tomorrow is Day One of the Lycian Way, the Likya Yolu in Turkish, and despite hundreds of YouTube videos— how-to tie knots, how-to read a compass, how-to use GPS on a cell phone—I am still in kindergarten. First day of kindergarten. Before recess.

Who am I to go on this journey?

I don't have that answer yet.

DAY 1

Ovacik to Faralya

I SWIPE MY CELL'S BLINKING clock left towards the ZZZs, and my dream continues in 15 minute episodes, where I dig in the sand for an overdue library book. My t-shirt hangs on the wooden chair—will it be warm enough? Should I move the sleeping bag back to the bottom of the pack? Do I need three bras? And what exactly is that extra six-inch metal tube in my tent bag?

Seven hours to Faralya, camping by 2:30pm.

I crawl across the bed to my double-layer wool socks and stand on the tiles to make sense of the shower—my last for a while—before I dress in my only set of hiking clothes and drop the key at the empty front desk.

"Okay, this is it," I say to Hotel Dog as I bend to twirl his ear between my fingers. As my knees creak straight, I peek behind me at Baba Dağ—Father Mountain—who towers over me. I tighten my pack's left strap and loosen the right. Hotel Dog blinks and tilts his head, one way, then the other. "Okay, you're right, I'll be fine."

Three red hens pop-and-lock down the hill with me, but stop short of the main road.

"Okay, here I go."

I walk on the left sidewalk to avoid the tourists in tank tops and flip flops who stare and point and laugh as they sip fresh-squeezed orange juice on patios across the empty street.

Ha. Oh look at you and your backpack, how long you've been hiking?

Um, 3.2 seconds.

You'll never make 500 kilometres.

But, I, uh, finished the West Coast Trail last year, that was 75 kilometres.

Whatever. You won't finish—

Hey, wait a minute. This is MY imagination. So I can stop it too. I block the mockery by making them gag. Just a little bit.

The tiny market I visited last night is now dark. Should I wait until it opens? I could buy another apple? Do I need more snacks? My stomach gurgles, not even wanting to eat the food I've packed for the day.

Three litres in the hydration pack stuffed inside my backpack no longer seems ridiculous as I wipe sweat from my forehead. I'm undecided about the two extra 400-millilitre plastic water bottles I packed at the last minute. However, I abandon the empty one next to a garbage can after two minutes of it knocking against my pack: click-clack, click-clack, click-clack.

The down-sloping concrete sidewalks go left at the roundabout before ending at a T-intersection.

"Likya Yolu?" I ask a man raking in a yard. Am I saying that right? Lick-ee-ya Yo-luu? He points right, then left. I bow my head with a slow blink, offering a smile instead of the six-syllable Turkish thank-you.

Cracked vertical pavement challenges my Achilles as my neck hyperextends so my eyes can roll up, in search of the top—wait, is that it? On the pole? It welcomes me like a friend-of-a-friend at a foreign airport. I press the middle of the thick white paint and slide my fingers down to pause on the red, tracing the ridges of the brush strokes over the smooth wood.

"Hi Likya."

My chest tightens. I'm really here.

Around the bend, in the silence of the woods, I stop under the yellow Likya Yolu/Lycian Way trail head arch and pull the bandana up from around my neck to wipe away tears, before reaching out to take a first photo.

I had debated taking any camera at all. Would I write if I took photographs too? Would I experience (and record) the moments differently if I only had a pen?

"If I uninstall my phone's camera, can I add it again later?" I had asked tech support.

"Why would you want to do that?" she asked.

"Um, a little radical simplicity, I just don't want to tempt myself with the option."

"If you don't want to do something, why don't you just not do it?"

"If only everything was that easy," I said.

I didn't delete the camera app. But I made the intention to focus on writing and bought a writing journal covered in photographs of cameras.

My boots shoot rocks like Tiddlywinks off the cliffs above Ölü Deniz, a pie-slice beach town of white houses, red roofs and blue-dot swimming pools. Turkish gulets—traditional wooden sailing vessels—prowl the water's edge for tourists. Thirty-one paragliders float like campfire ashes. As I pass two cisterns, I haul up the concrete lids and check—both full.

Through the farming village of Kirme, cows pose like antique portraits from doorways and windows of half-built cement houses. Sweat soon evaporates as gravity lures me down a steep winding road. My arms swing loose for the next half hour, and my mind wanders back to the tourists gagging on their orange juice.

"Look at me now, hiii-king in Tuuur-key, so eeeasy," I say. "Hey, chicken, why you crossing the road?"

It rolls its eyes and jerks into the driveway towards a villager who straightens from her sweeping position and pulls down the black sleeveless vest across her baggy, floral pants.

"*Günaydin*! Good morning!" I say with a wave.

"Günaydin," she says and smiles.

I want to share a chicken joke but only know three words: Why? *Neden*. Chicken? Nope. Meat? *Et*. Road? *Yol*.

I blink and squint at a black object on the road.

"Euww, what, the hell?" A goat leg, hoof still attached. Nine years as a police officer taught me to laugh in the presence of unattached body parts.

A foot-long leg? I unzip my hip pocket to get my camera/phone.

Nah. Nothing to see here folks, move along. Body-shutters propel me down the hill even faster.

Hey, wait a minute. It's been too long without a sign. Where does this road even go? My map shows the white line leading to the coast, then connecting to a yellow highway, away from Faralya. For the first time on the trail, I check my phone's GPS. The orange hang glider you-are-here shape floats all alone in the grey background, and the red waypoint line is invisible. Shit. I look uphill. Downhill. Day one. Lost. How far off am I? Do I stay on the road and meet up with the trail later? What sign did I miss? How did I go wrong? I turn around. Arms still. Head down. Sweat polishes my boots as I climb. I get to the goat leg and step around it.

"Yeah, I get it now, you were the sign, I shouldn't have passed you."

At the chicken's driveway, I wave to the elderly woman.

"*Merhaba*. Hello. Likya?" She points to the hill and starts walking up. My open palms reject her kindness, but she slaps my hands away, giggles, and we walk side-by-side up the hill. Ten minutes later, she stops and sighs.

"Yeah, it is hot," I say. She pats my backpack, and I guess at her short question in Turkish, holding up ten fingers and then five again to mime the weight of my pack. Her eyebrows lift. My doubts need this, somebody to be impressed, proud of me. I want to hug her.

We step onto a red dirt single-track, and she speaks fast while her arms exaggerate turns, a left, a right and a left again.

"Thank you so much. Te-shey—" I mumble and she finishes the last four syllables, "ker-i-der-im."

Together we laugh as my attempts improve from non-existent to the ridiculous. I turn back after 30 feet to see her watching me. I wave and she swings her arm wide to the right. I go right, and a red and white paint swoosh on a rock confirms her wisdom.

"Hi Likya," and a back-up check of my GPS agrees. The orange you-are-here marker is no longer floating alone in the greyness but back on the red jagged trail line.

Parallel to the trail, a dozen blue box bee hives line up unevenly on the grass field. Behind me, goat bells, and below at my feet, a grey and olive green tortoise, the size of a dinner plate. I'm done with body parts. Bring on the animals.

The cliff top village of Faralya greets me in the early afternoon, and I fill my water at a public sink next to the mosque. There's also a toilet. A squat toilet. I scan the empty street, but my sunburned cheeks feel more heat anyways. For over 40 years, I've squatted in the woods while camping. I've hovered over shit-filled toilets in remote Mexican bus stations, and I've waded through urine-covered floors in Thai huts. Why am I anxious about my first squat toilet? But do I fill that small bucket with water and throw it down the hole after I go? Throw it between my legs? Do I use my toilet paper? Where do I put it after? Without giving the anxiety the time to grow, I lean my pack against the sink, walk inside and close the door.

I am both hungry and not at all, but unsure of my next food source, I order a take-out sandwich at a roadside café. I have no energy, or confidence, to practice the Turkish language or cultural customs. Instead, I long for the comfort and solitude of my tent. While I wait, I scan the half-full outdoor patio overlooking Butterfly Valley. Do I climb down to the beach?

The path drops abruptly over the face of the cliff, I reread in Kate Clow's *The Lycian Way*, the only guidebook available. My previous adventure on the West Coast Trail had 67 ladders—moss-covered, worn out, 60-foot ladders—nailed into cliffs hanging over the ocean, and I had discovered a fear of heights halfway up the first ladder.

Even with ropes, the path is dangerous, a fall in the wrong place could be fatal. I don't even try to look for the trail head to the beach.

My sandwich drums on the outside of my pack as I march out of Faralya and soon leave the paved road for a narrow trail of boulder stairs. Within a minute, goose bumps flick the sweat off my arms, and I shiver as one shaky hand braces against a rock, the other covers my mouth. Too much sun? Not enough food? Ten minutes later, the shivers stop, the nausea disappears and I wobble up the hill.

I stop at the first flat area in a half-hour—a small clearing off the trail. Will this work? I drop my pack in the open area and walk back through the bush to the trail. Nope, I can still see it. I bushwhack further off the trail to another tiny clearing and check again from the trail. Hidden. I don't want to be seen by anyone. Yet I don't want to be alone, in the dark, where the mind writes horror stories from noises at midnight.

I set up my one-person tent against the trunk of a pine tree just as warm rain starts. Inside, I change from sweat-soaked hiking clothes into dry camp clothes—black nylon running shorts, billowy black short-sleeve cotton shirt, and $4 flip-flops—and string up the wet clothes from the roof of my tent. Next, I unroll my Therm-a-Rest self-inflating sleeping pad and fold it into the Therm-a-Rest nylon chair kit—my essential buddy on the Greek islands, Mexican beaches and the West Coast Trail. The chair sleeve weighs 11 ounces, but I'll defend it with honour to anyone who suggests it be left out in favour of a lighter pack. But after day one, I do reconsider other things, and hold each item as I decide: a black tank top? The extra shirt for town? Third bra and underwear? Gone gone gone. Flannel stuff sack to create a pillow? What about my one plastic plate? Gone. The purpose-specific solar battery case stays the longest in my hands. But all non-essentials. I'd later regret tossing one small luxury, the tiny salt and pepper shaker, but only for a moment.

As rain pings off the nylon roof, I recline in my chair, legs straight out and write in my camera-covered journal while eating the best tomato-cucumber-cheese sandwich ever. I didn't eat all day, couldn't eat, until now. Why? The essentials: gas, food, lodging. Water was easy to find today, but a full three-litre water bag didn't stop me checking every source. Did I need to find more food, have an emergency stash, before I could eat the ration for today? Did I need to confirm a place to sleep before I could relax enough to eat? I need another way.

By 5 o'clock, the rain stops. Body and mind rested, I stretch my legs while walking through the woods and find a clearing the size of a baseball field, with sunshine and mountain views. Even though it is exposed and closer to the trail, I move camp. Once I'm set up again, three people walk into the clearing—the first people I've seen on the trail all day—a Russian couple on the trail for two weeks and a Turkish woman joining them for two nights as she tries camping for the first time. We swap stories and laugh through the sunset, and I fall asleep as their tents bookend mine, my first night of wild camping.

DAY 2

Faralya to Alinca

AT 5:30, THE CALL TO PRAYER welcomes the morning. The other two tents are silent and I argue with myself for an hour. Lay still and keep quiet? Pack up and go but make noise? Finally, I pack up, sleeping bag on the bottom this time and the rest of the items burrow into their rightful places.

Along the downhill path, anonymous angry Turkish interrupts non-stop barking. In contrast, my rampage of gratitude for my height-adjustable pants continues as prickles snag my pant legs. The taller prickles grate my sunburned arms. I might have to change to a long-sleeve—"shiii-it!" My non-essentials wait under the tree of my first campsite; hopefully someone will find a gift instead of litter. Sorry, Turkey.

An hour up the trail, a man and woman sell orange juice and whole apples in a tin-roof hut.

"Günaydin," I say.

"Günaydin. Yes?" the man asks as he points to a basket of oranges.

"*Evet*, yes." I drop my pack and wait on a makeshift bench next to a wood stove, the size and shape of a beer keg. Two kettles simmer on top, a tray of tulip tea glasses rests on the ground, and a view of the sea completes the moment.

He slices an orange and muscles the mechanical press—slice, squeeze, pour—until a glass fills.

"How are you?" he asks.

As I sip the juice, I can only moan ohhh, mmm, ohhh, and the woman, in village uniform of head scarf, sleeveless cardigan sweater and baggy floral pants, giggles. We chat and mime over tea and orange juice before it's time to move on.

"Te-shey-ker-a-dir-im, thank you" I say. "And goodbye?"

"*Güle güle,*" she says as she points to herself and, "*hoşçakal*" as she points to me.

"You say, goo-lay goo-lay and I say, hosh-chak-al."

She nods and whispers, "Güle güle, hoşçakal."

The vacant trail cuts through wheat fields and pine forests for another hour until Likya requires a decision—right for Kabak Beach, left to Alinca. Just then, two men with full packs walk up, the first hikers this morning.

"Günaydin, do you speak English?"

"A little," one says.

"Where are you going?"

"To Alinca then Bel," the other man says, with an accent.

"Me too. And you are from Italy?"

"*Si, si.*"

I let them go first as I sip my water in the shade. I've always had this annoyance about following somebody who has merged onto the same trail, at the same pace. But come towards me? I'll smile and wave and be thrilled to see you.

The murmur of trilled Rs hovers at each switchback. Knowing they are only a bend away, I teach myself a slower pace, a new way that becomes a welcome habit the next four weeks.

I overtake the Italians when they stop to chat with other Italians and no one else joins for hours. The trail climbs to Alinca along red cliffs that drop a hundred feet just a few long strides off the trail.

At the end of the second hour, hikers holding tiny plastic water bottles appear—first a trickle, then a gush. "Günaydin! Hello!" I soon add more vocabulary to guess their home countries within our three second connection: "Günaydin! Bonjour! Guten morgen! Buenos dias! Buongiorno!" A few answers are unrecognizable. The trail is busy and the number of waymarks matches the number of tourists—I wonder which came first.

The medium-size names on my map are villages that have houses, a café, and maybe a market, maybe a *pansiyon*, a small guesthouse. As I walk through Alinca, there are the houses, there is the pansiyon, and then the trail leaps over the mountainside. What about water? Food? I turn around and ask a woman on the street, "*Su var?* There is water there?" She points to a blank two-story white building. I mime a tap and ask again, "su?" With the same gentle smile, she again points to the building, no hint of annoyance at my disbelief. In somebody's house? I can't just walk into somebody's house for water. I check today's route again—no cisterns—and my body won't let me leave Alinca without water. I walk towards the building but pause for more forceful guidance. The man in the yard points to another man at the bottom of the stairs, who points to another man at the top of the stairs. I follow the man-trail and—a café deck! Water. Food. Sit.

"Where did you start? Kabak?" he asks in English.

"Ovacik."

"Oh!" and smiles as he parachutes a clean floral cloth onto a table. Empty wooden chairs painted blue share my view to the sea, how do I choose one of 15 perfect seats?

The menu has photos and I point to a salad, and soup.

"*Et?*" I ask.

"Nooo."

"*Sebze?*" I don't know how to say vegetarian but the two words I did practice—meat and vegetable—somewhat work. He scrunches his face and follows my finger down my list of Turkish words.

"Ah, sebze. Yes, vegetables."

"Su?"

He walks out of sight and boomerangs with two large bottles of water.

"Teşekkür ederim, thank you."

A few minutes later a woman—the same woman I asked on the road—delivers the vegetable soup, basket of inch-cut white bread and a salad of tomato, cucumbers and long, thin green peppers cut into rounds with seeds still inside. Without tasting first, I pick up the salt shaker—beautiful, chunky sea salt—and here, here's that moment. But, wait. Is it regret, of not having? Or is it gratitude, of having? With leftover oil and vinegar dressing, I sink all six pieces of bread in the shallow end. I gulp the water during lunch but there's still enough to fill my water pack plus the small, extra water bottle. Ooo, a bath. And laundry too?

For the next hour, my boots clomp down the abrupt terraces as the bread in my gut weights me to the sharp-angled trail like the egg-shaped Weeble. A few hikers with day packs pass me and more are up ahead on the switchbacks. No one's camping. No flat spots anyways. Wait. There? An area the size of my tent's footprint is a long jump off the trail but under dark shade. I walk on. But slower. There? It's 20 feet beyond the switchback curve, so people wouldn't be walking right by tent. Not bad, not great. Keep going?

I dip into the pine forest for another possible option. It doesn't feel right. But right at the trail sign pointing to the village of Gey, a bright field with views of the sea, a single shade tree and wandering goats. Perfect.

I set my sleeping pad chair in the shade and before I change out of my sweaty hiking clothes, I sit. Sit and watch the goats. Sit and stare at the sea. Twenty minutes go by until the lactic acid build-up in my lower limbs compels me to explore my campground.

"Hi, I heard your English and wanted to come say hello," I say to three women at the Likya/Gey signpost.

"Where did you come from?" one woman asks.

"Today, Faralya".

"And you're by yourself?" asks another.

"Yes, and where are you all from?"

"I'm from Germany."

"I'm from India."

"I'm from Switzerland, but we all live in Istanbul and met at work."

We chat a few minutes before I wish them well. It's bath time.

After changing into my camp clothes, I fill a large, resealable freezer bag with 400 millilitres of water, a few drops of liquid soap and swish. First, my underwear. Then I use my clean underwear to wash salt and dirt from my face and neck, then feet, legs and lower arms and finally, under my shirt for my upper arms, underarms and torso. It's true, a Turkish bath is luxurious. Enough water remains, so I wash my bra, t-shirt and wool socks. The pants won't fit and will have to wait.

My limbs air dry in the sun as I watch goats graze. Three generations of conversation—the old goat, the patient adults and the kids that, more than once, cause my head to snap around and search for the wailing human baby. Chatter fades as they move down the hill. Silence.

Given my history of lighting stoves on fire, (yeah, you read that right) I had decided not to bring a camp stove. My enthusiasm for camping seems to thrive despite my inability to build a fire, prime a camp stove or hang a tarp. Yes, friends have explained it all to me. Instructors have taught it all to me. YouTube has shown it all to me. Repeatedly. The knowledge lasts all of 3.2 seconds. But I'm excellent at making-do. I stuff white cheese into a hunk of bread and nod off during the chocolate chip cookie dessert. Can I sleep with the sun still up?

I scan the pine forest behind the field and when I pull a toilet paper roll from its plastic bag, two condoms full out.

Oh jesus. I had stayed with a friend close to the airport and she had thrown them into my bathroom supplies while I re-packed a third time.

"I'm hiking, on my own," I said. "This is not about men."

"You never know," she said.

As I tumble out of the woods, a man jogs across the field. I barely get my used toilet paper into its odour-proof bag and thrown into my tent when he's close enough to introduce himself.

"Welcome!" he says in English. "Yusuf, shepherd."

"Merhaba, Yusuf. Michelle, Canada."

And for the next hour we talk with my little Turkish, his little English (learned from tourists) plus mime, dirt doodles and Google Translate:

"How many goats do you have?"

"One hundred."

"You have a dog to help?"

"No."

"How do you know your goats?"

"Yellow plastic in ear."

"Only your goats have a yellow tag?"

"All goats."

"But how do you know it's your goat?"

"By their face."

"Where do goats stay?"

"In a goat house, two hundred metres away."

"You walk to get them and lead to the goat house?

"Yes, and call them."

" Do other shepherds use dogs?"

"Some."

He holds out a pack of TEKEL 2001. I pinch a filter and slide a cigarette from the fresh deck, lean into his flame and inhale deep. What, I smoke now?

After smoking through high school, I first quit in university as part of a Psychology 201 project. *Your paper smells like smoke*, the professor wrote in red pen beside the A+ grade. I quit for good during the next semester. Ten years later, I used cigarettes when working as an undercover drug buyer in Vancouver's downtown eastside. The sellers would look for the un-police-like nicotine stains on your teeth and fingers and my theatrical make-up felt more believable when paired with a real prop. And not being a good liar, the cigarettes helped dissipate my nerves—holding them, inhaling them, twirling them. Smoking once or twice a month, the habit never took hold, and I might still be a once-a-month smoker if I knew any smokers at home.

I'm not sure why I accept Yusuf's offer of a cigarette but as I sit under a tree with my first Turkish shepherd, sharing our days, it feels normal, and right.

"I love dogs," he says when I show him Monty's photo on my phone.

"Doberman?"

"Rottweiler. He died."

"Ohhh."

"When in Canada, I get another dog."

"Oh good."

"You know Likya Yolu to Gey?"

"Yes."

"Steep cliffs?"

"No, it's okay."

"My book says very steep cliffs."

"No."

"After Gey?"

"No."

He points to where I had come from earlier today.

"Are you sure?

"Yes."

"Only back there?"

"Yes."

"Okay, trust the *çoban*, trust the shepherd. Right?"

"Yes, good, thank you."

His cell phone rings, a young child's voice.

"Your baby?"

"Yes, son, two daughters, you?"

"No, only dogs."

He laughs. "I am 40."

"I am 45."

"You married?"

"Yes, he's in Canada." I twirl my second cigarette.

"Why?"

"I holiday, he work." Twirl. Twirl. Twirl.

After chatting about tourists, sheep versus goats and Turkish vocabulary, we say goodnight and Yusuf leaves to collect his goats.

Forty minutes later, my pen stops mid-sentence. Footsteps.

"Michelle?"

"Hel-looo!"

By the time I crawl out of my tent, he's spread out his coat and on top, his dinner to share. The tremendous kindness, which seems an everyday gesture for Yusuf, obliterates my default reaction of refusal. How can I say no to this? Together, we practice our second languages as we break bread and scoop tomato and pepper sauce. He insists leaving me some for breakfast and shows me how to leave the container and plastic bag tied to the tree for him to pick up later.

"Güle güle, Yusuf, and teşekkür ederim, thank you."

"Goodbye, Michelle," he says. "I honk goodnight, on my motorcycle."

I brush my teeth and then tunnel deep into my sleeping bag—beep-beep, beep-beep—and flip off my headlamp.

DAY 3

Alinca to Gavuraǧili

AT 2 O'CLOCK IN THE MORNING, it makes itself known. It blasts in from the far left, hovers in front and disappears to the right in a manic pirouette. It returns again and again, causing my tent walls to squeeze me tighter and tighter. I'll listen to its howls from inside, but no eye contact. Ignore it? Well, that pisses it off. The fury peaks at 6:05am when it sinks in its teeth and rips out the vestibule peg, leaving the nylon door to flail back and forth.

"Alright, alright. F-uuck!"

I stomp out of the tent and tear off the fly but it snatches it mid-air and I barely snag the last inch to reel it back in. I lug my backpack out of the tent and heave it one-handed on top of the fly. Without me or my backpack inside, my featherweight dwelling inflates (note: always peg a tent), but I snap off the poles left-handed and collapse it. With everything flat and still for a millisecond, I run off to pee. But while crouching behind bushes, I watch it flip and eviscerate my tent.

"F-uuck!"

I shuffle-hop out of the bushes, pants still around my ankles and swan dive to hang on tighter than little Carol Anne's mom in that possessed bedroom closet.

It's not the first time I've been chased out of a campsite by possessed wind. During another Mexican road trip, a friend and I stopped in Gorman, California—elevation 4000 feet. We awoke as it dragged our tent across the sandy dirt, with a 33-quart cooler, and us, still in it. We fought back with curse words and laughter and seventeen years later, the photo of the demonized tent still ignites giggles.

What do you do when all your belongings are folded inside a nylon burrito and topped with a half-fuming, half-giggling hiker? I don't know either. I wiggle back into my pants and transition to 100 percent laughing. Good thing I already peed.

"Oh yeah? Bring it on!"

I reach underneath and through the door, a blind search for the sleeping bag, but instead a palm-size piece of paper shoots out as if from a confetti cannon. Shit! I loathe litter but won't risk all my belongings for a recovery mission. Sorry again, Turkey.

I stick my hand under and feel around again, like that Price Is Right game where contestants reach in a droopy bag and pull out oversized poker chips. It's... a... phone! And.... a .... journal! An MP3 player ... and .... headphones! I slide out the soft item that I've been using as a knee pad. A hunk of bread.

Everything has to fit into the backpack a certain way—sleeping bag on bottom, clothes fill in tiny spaces like sand—or things poke into your back.

My baseball cap blows off my head three times but catches in my mass of bed-head ponytail. My scarf! I slam my half-filled backpack onto the tent and sprint 30 feet across the sharp rocks to seize it mid-air.

Toilet paper roll? Into the front pocket. Maps? Side pocket. Bandana? Around my neck.

Shit! More confetti. I hunt for these critical bits of paper. Until I find a pocket-size notebook, it's all I have to write my memories of the trail.

Only the tent itself remains. I reach in—grab the tent bag— stuff the tent in—triple-clip the bag—tighten the straps—flip it over—a-ha!—thrust my hand into the air to signal victory.

Yusuf appears. He wants to show me his goats and introduce his wife. I dig into my ramshackle pack and present a teeny gift—a Canadian flag. After pinning it to his jacket, he rests a hand over his heart, straightens his back and bows his head—until the wind plucks off his baseball cap and whips it across the field.

We walk Likya together until he points to a tidy stone house and his wife standing outside, "Goat house," he says. He points to a makeshift shack with a blue tarp roof, "My house." After good-bye waves and smiles, I continue on solo. Within minutes, I'm lost, and I miss Yusuf's trail knowledge. No sign. No waymark. GPS? The waypoints display but my location doesn't. Can't build a fire, can't prime a camp stove, can't hang a tarp, and oh yeah, can't make sense of GPS.

I had tried downloading local trail waypoints to practice. Nope. I had searched for orienteering workshops. None available. I had posted an ad on Craigslist for a private tutor. No response. GPS in the car? No problem. Build my company's website with integrated e-commerce? Sure. Set up and operate my entire global business online? Doing it. But trail GPS? I just don't get it. Right up there with sailing, poker and American football. *GPS is a luxury, although it can save you time when you are lost,* says my guidebook. But I still want it. The rock-solid guidance. I thought I would need it. So I persisted. I pushed. I can't explain, or even remember, how I managed to finally download someone's waypoints into a GPS app. A map overlay? Non-existent. Only red waypoints dotting randomly across a blank grey screen with an orange triangle you-

are-here icon—so *turn right at the next street* or *cross that stream* aren't
options—but at least I'll know if I'm in the rough vicinity of the
trail.

I tuck away my inept cell phone. I walk 200 feet to the right. No
signs. I walk back to the intersection and go 200 feet left. No signs.
As I stand staring into the fallen leaves, unable to decide, the
ground moves—grasshoppers. Left? Right? Which way guys? I
choose right again, and 30 feet down the trail, a red and white
waymark waves. How'd I miss that?

My mind sleeps as my body propels forward on its own,
without interruption by other hikers. A dirt road leads the three
kilometres into Gey, and my poles create a tripod to keep my 140-
pound body and 28-pound pack upright in the wind. Stone houses
and empty fields wind up to the village market. Inside, about the
size of a bedroom, the market has full shelves of crackers,
tomatoes, cucumbers, coffee, rice, pasta and honey plus safety pins,
sanitary napkins (no tampons) and batteries. Amongst the beer,
pop and water, I select an iced tea, roll of graham crackers, semi-
soft cheese, and it's here I discover the mind-blowing *yufka*—a thin,
round unleavened flat bread, a foot-and-a-half in diameter.

I chat with two older women from Germany. They are hiking
east too but staying in pansiyons each night.

"And what about the steep cliffs coming up?" I ask.

"We don't know yet, we're staying here tonight."

I want to study their detailed map, purchased in Fethiye, but
they leave while I buy a second iced tea.

For 500 metres, the route is narrow and runs above a high and steep slope,
people who don't like heights may be worried. You should not do this section in
bad weather, I read for the third time. Windy? Check. Rain? Not yet,
but dark clouds hang low. What if I bust an ankle? What if the wind
blows me off the cliff? What if I reach a level of fear that freezes

me in place like a gecko? I'd look like an asshole. *It said don't do in the wind or rain! It said not for people with fear of heights!*

While training for long-distance trail races in local mountains, my running buddy and I would, at times, find ourselves running knee-deep in snow and one of us would say, "We'd better not end up on the front page of the newspaper because of a rescue. We'd look like assholes." But we knew that trail system inside-out, we knew our location at every moment (well, mostly) and we always stuck together. Here? I have none of that.

I study my map for an alternative route—a white line signalling a double-track tractor path—to my destination of Bel. But if I go off the trail, there'd be no GPS waypoints. No Likya guidance. No hikers. My dad and sister know the name of the Lycian Way, but because I don't check in, they don't know my daily route. No one does. I have the local search and rescue phone numbers. But cell service? If something happens anywhere on the Likya trail itself, it may take several hours or several days but eventually (that's my plan) someone will come along—a hiker, a shepherd. But if I take the alternate route, an unknown and possibly abandoned trail, would there be anyone? I drink my second iced tea in half-sips, quarter-sips. Steep cliffs or isolation?

"Dolmuş?" I ask the shopkeeper.

"No," she says.

No bus, hiking it is then. Which way? Road. Yes, road. Road? Maybe the trail isn't that narrow? How steep is steep?

It's late morning, I must go. I walk through the quiet village to the Likya signpost—the Likya path to Bel goes right. I turn left.

"Bel *yol*, Bel road?" I ask a man.

"Evet," he says.

I ask a second man.

"Evet," he says.

I ask a third man.

"Evet," he says and nods his head.

I point to my watch. He holds up two fingers then a third finger which he slashes in half. Two-and-a-half hours. He doesn't look nervous for me. He doesn't try to talk me out of it. He's probably walked it too. Deciding on a path—of two unknown paths—and moving forward allows my chest to loosen. Somewhat.

The rocky, double-track tractor path cuts through the mountain. I hope it's a single direction with no splits, but decide in advance to always choose right, right towards the sea. After a half-hour of looking over my shoulder, I need a technique to re-create a comfort zone. Music always helps. A little INXS. Or Florence and the Machine. Maybe Stereophonics. Yes! Stereophonics. I dig out my MP3 player from my backpack and unravel the headphones. No power. I hold the ON button twice as long. Nothing. Again. It had a full battery yesterday. "Oh, come on, work with me, I need tunes." Nothing. "F-uuck!" I wrap the headphones around the matchbook-size unit—more aerodynamic when I throw it—but stop when I imagine it boomeranging as a penalty for my outburst. I know if it doesn't work, I'm supposed to be in silence. But I don't have to like it.

"Okay, f-iiine," I mutter and stuff it in a cargo pocket. "Stupid MP3."

The climb continues to 800 metres, and a slice in the mountain offers a sea view. My eyes focus on the dense treetops below. Sheer cliff drops? That pencil-line goat trail, is that it? Wait, am I on the right road? Is this the way? Have I missed a turn? A sign, any sign, is welcome. Down an embankment, a black and white cow with yellow ear tags chews cud. I imitate. "Hi cow!" Behind the cow, a man stands up.

"Oh, uh, hello, merhaba."

He drops his shovel and scrambles up the mound.

"Hoş geldiniz!" he yells as his hands envelope mine. His huge smile reveals crooked, stained teeth the colour of his sun-darkened skin.

"Canada!"

"Ah!" he says as he pumps my arms.

"Bel?"

"Evet."

I reach into my left cargo pocket, my map's home. Empty. I spin around and scan the road. Did it fall out when I fiddled with my MP3 player? No trail. No GPS. No map. Was it right at the fork? Or was it go left? He reads my thoughts and mimes a fork in the road, taps his right arm and drifts it right like a ballet dancer, "Bel." He taps his left arm and drifts it left, "Sidyma."

"Kilometres? Bel?"

He taps my watch at 6-7-8-9.

"Fifteen kilometres?" I ask as I open and close my hand three times.

"Evet."

"Kilometres?"

"Evet."

"Hours?"

He holds up three fingers.

I inhale deep and exhale slow. He smiles. I don't. I don't have water for three more hours. Did I miss a turn? A goat path? His enormous goodbye wave pushes me forward.

At the fork, a lady waves, standing amongst chickens in her yard.

"Merhaba, Bel?"

She points to her left, my right.

I walk down around switchbacks and into the village of Bel. Not 15 kilometres. Fifteen minutes.

To reach the public water fountain, I step onto a wooden platform built around a tree, with benches lining the edges. A village woman waddles by, with wide strands of wheat or barley stacked high so only her sandals are visible from the back. She stops to rest against the stone wall adjacent to the dirt road.

"Merhaba," she says.

"Merhaba. Su, Belceiz?"

"*Hayır*, Belceiz," she says as she slashes the air.

Got it. No water in the next village. I'll fill up here.

"*Çay?*" a woman calls out, leaning from a window in the building behind.

"Evet, teşekkür ederim." A tea? Oh yes, thank you.

She greets me at the taps, and I follow her through a wrought iron gate and into the lower floor of her home. There are no walls. Beyond, lies a back and side yard green with plants. An open fire hosts a large black cauldron. Another woman points to one of four wooden chairs, and one plastic, around a wooden table. She ducks through a curtain and returns with a two-tier silver teapot—a çaydanlik. From the top, she pours dark tea into a tulip glass and from the bottom pot, hot water completes the fill. Sugar is in a green plastic bowl.

As the tea meets my lips, the call to prayer floats through the room. On only the third day of my month-long hike, I'm sipping tea, in a villager's home, on a mountain top, in Turkey. I get 26 more days like this? Without the words to explain my gratitude, or watery eyes, I simply let the experience flow through me.

A man joins us, and a cat too, curling up on the plastic chair.

"Köpek?" I ask and point to the cat. If I say dog, I'll learn cat.

"Kedi."

"Kedi kedi kedi, kitty kitty kitty. Kedi, Canada?" I pretend to stuff the cat under my arm. "Kedi, çay?" Tea for the cat? There's a Cat Stevens joke in there somewhere.

"Hayir!" they all laugh.

"Köpek, Bel?"

The woman holds up five fingers. I want to find one of Bel's five dogs.

"Kedi?"

She points everywhere.

"Ah, kedi kedi kedi, köpek, kedi kedi kedi, woof."

"People?" I ask as I point to each person at the table.

Ninety-five.

Another half-hour of conversation via Google Translate, and it's time to go. I'm not sure if she expects or even wants money. But I'm not yet used to Turkey's generosity and feel the urge to reciprocate with payment. I offer her three lira in coins, about what I'd pay in Canada. She shrugs and says thank you. I'm uncertain if I've offended her generosity, embarrassed her or underpaid but we say goodbye with handshakes and smiles.

Crunch—clack—bop. My feet, my poles and my full plastic water bottle hanging from a carabiner. Crunch—clack—bop. A puffed up turkey interrupts the percussion when he struts across the road. I can relate, buddy. That unknown road all felt easy, even enjoyable, now that I'm at the end, in Bel. But I still prefer the company of Likya. When the first red and white waymark waves from a rock just out of town my gut crunches and I inhale deep. I'm back, Likya, so nice to see you again.

The trail veers off the road into a dense forest and soon opens to a flat terrace—a great camping spot—but it's only 2 o'clock. My puffed-turkey-confidence keeps me moving and for the next two hours, my Vibram soles suck on sharp-angled boulders. Waymarks lounge on flat rocks every 100 feet or so. If I don't see one, I shift left or right and there it is. Oh Likya, you mess with me.

Long-distance views provide the back-drop, but the sea blends with the sky, creating a bizarre blue vortex. I haven't seen anyone in two hours, and a lone white dot sailing provides the only evidence of humans. White caps stop. Clouds remain. It's nice to not have ass-sweat today. But my feet burn, and tenderness builds as I trade boulders for thumb-size jagged rocks. By the time a semi-flat area the size of my tent shows up, it's 4 o'clock.

The ritual develops and extends—change into camp clothes, recline on the sleeping pad, prop bare feet against a cool, vertical rock surface, nibble crackers and sip water, drop arms to the sides like a T. Eyes gaze into the sky, or thick leaves, in this case.

Gas. Food. Lodging. And goats.

After 30 minutes, I set up the tent, hang up sweaty clothes and make a dinner of cucumbers and soft cream cheese on Yusuf's mushed bread.

I check my MP3 player—it works. I love you, MP3.

By 6:30pm, I sit and write. Goat bells increase in tone and volume until it's like a wind chime test factory. My pen shakes as my giggles match the crescendo of the goats' cries. "Oh-hey," bellows the shepherd. By 9 o'clock, the goats travel up the path in the dim light, a few stop and stare. How close would they come? I want to pat a goat. The goats are aloof, but the shepherd isn't. His name is Yusuf too. I learn more Turkish during the next ten minutes:

"Your goats?"

"No goat, sheep."

Oops.

How many?"

"Fifty-two."

"What time do they sleep?"

He points to my watch. "Now."

"*Ev?* House?"

"Yes."

We say goodbye, and as I tuck myself into bed, I imagine the sheep tucked into theirs.

DAY 4

Gavurağili to Xanthos

RAIN KEPT THE NIGHT HUMID, and I dozed on top of my sleeping bag, skin sticky with three days of salt. Red ants the weight of eyelashes tiptoed around their unfamiliar surroundings (and me) all night. Because it was the only area without sharp rocks, the noticeable slant didn't register during set-up, and I had squeezed my tent in-between a tree and a two foot high drop-off. But with a nylon sleeping bag and smooth sleeping pad, it was an all-night ride on The Scrambler. Annoying enough to disturb sleep but not annoying enough to get up and do something about it.

I crave oranges, but in the meantime I review today's laminate map over a breakfast of graham crackers and cheese. Hiking the Lycian? Laminate. I had photocopied the map included in *The Lycian Way* guidebook—creating one 8 ½ x 11 inch section for each day's route—plus elevation graphs and portions of the guidebook's narrative which I taped to the back. Lamination cost me twice the price of the book, but it was worth it for the protection against rain and heavy use. And it doubles as a plate too. Now, I could focus on only one day at a time, a small thing my fatigued brain embraced.

Today's route? The elevation graphs shows flat after the initial two kilometres. *Easy route,* says the book. Good, because I'm irritable this morning. And my tired body needs an easy day.

On the outer edges of the tiny village of Gavurağili, a group of campers stand around an open fire, the first campers I've met since starting.

"Merhaba!"

"Hello!" say two guys while the other three people wave.

"Do you have a map?" asks Vladimir.

"Yes, did you lose your map?"

"No, we only took a photo of the map right at the start."

All from Russia, Masha, Vladimir, Julia and Yura have only two more days, but a second Vladimir will return to Antalya and onwards to Cappadocia.

"You are travelling alone?" he asks.

"Yes."

"And you are hiking the whole way?"

"Yep."

"Oh, you are my hero," he said in a low tone while bowing his head. "But this is not your first time?"

"Not my first time travelling solo, but my first time hiking and camping solo."

"Wow. Here, want an orange?"

"Oh thank you. And is there a tap for water?" I ask. Starting the day with full water is one less worry.

"I'll show you," says Yura.

We bushwhack through a barely-there trail to a spigot sticking out of a moss-covered stone wall. Drips fall into a concrete cistern. For goats?

"How on earth did you find this?"

36

"We explored the area by moonlight, and our lamps," he says as he points to his forehead. "Things appear when you need them."

I scramble up a short forest trail and pop onto a road. Wait. Is that gushing water? Around a bend, a faucet runs full force into an overflowing cement basin the size of a bathtub. Instead of settling for goat water, had I waited, and trusted—a fresh geyser! The handle spins off in my hand. I pluck a plastic bag and piece of cloth from a litter pile and tie it around the faucet, but the water still surges, now like a lawn sprinkler. After a four minute shower, I give up. Sorry, Turkey.

A clear path leads off the road and opens wide across slanted boulders. My Vibram soles pucker up. Grasslands and farmlands paint the land across the road. Ruins, too. I'm not at all interested in historical architecture (did you just gasp?), but walking through random ruins in the middle of a Turkish countryside? Well, that's cool. Forty minutes on, the path ends on a tractor road. A red painted X on a rock on my right bounces me left. But it feels like I'm backtracking. I hate backtracking. Sure enough, here's Yura and Masha, two of the Russian campers.

"Hey! Where are you going?" Yura asks.

"I thought Xanthos," I say as I turn around.

Yura and Masha walk fast, so we say goodbye. I walk back over the slanted boulders and once on the road, I look left. How'd I miss that two-foot high rock cairn? I walk through the forest and duck through the low doorway of those same ruins that I had seen across the street from the trail (but didn't make the connection). The path narrows into a single-track and disappears in the tall grass. No waymarks. No path. A river and a lake displays on the map so I head towards the clearing to my right, seems like a lake area. By lunch time, a pedestrian bridge, made of thin boards nailed to trees straddling the river, leads to bungalows surrounding a restaurant. Outside, picnic tables wait for bums, and inside, a wall of booze waits for thirsty patrons.

"You camp?" yells a man.

"No, Letoon," I say. "*Yemek*? Food?" and point to the photos of the menu items above the bar.

"No, I don't have time," he mutters in English and walks away.

I grab a Coke, nectarine juice, small roll of chocolate chip cookies and two apples from the bare shelves.

"Twenty lira," he snaps.

In a rush to prevent this first-time grumpy energy from latching on to me, I drop a twenty lira note on the bar and bail. Later, in the mind-wandering solitude of walking, the foreign exchange calculates—nine bucks. Jerk.

Twelve-week-old puppies, two black, two white, flip and roll in the middle of the dead-end dirt road. After grieving my Rottweiler, Monty, for the past 15 months, my heart is open and eager for a dog to find me. I've pulled my car over to cuddle a yellow Labrador retriever puppy, I've lifted a French bulldog off a Vancouver city sidewalk without asking permission, and I may have shed a tear at a stuffed Bernese Mountain Dog in a pink baby stroller in a store window.

"Puppies puppies puppies!" I scream. "Puppies puppies puppies!"

I squat and all four ambush, my pack now an anchor.

"Puppies puppies puppies!"

The attack continues as my black pants marinate in the wet sand.

I peek at their patient mama ten feet away.

"Okay, okay, that's enough."

I walk and mama leads the way, puppies following. I now ignore them, hoping they'll turn back, which they do eventually. My daily map shows this as a one-road, flat walk of six kilometres, so I dig out my tunes. Shuffle mode starts with Scissor Sisters' "Laura", Guns N' Roses' cover of "Sympathy for the Devil", and The Dandy Warhols' "Bohemian Like You."

No cars. No people. Only me and loud musical geniuses. My walking poles drum and swing as I dance along a sandy track among mimosa scrub and eucalyptus trees—or so my guidebook says. Botanist I'm not.

The concert continues—Bob Geldof's "Mudslide", Sinéad O'Connor's "I Want Your Hands On Me", the Clash's "Train in Vain" and the Rolling Stones' "Beast of Burden," but Mick Jagger storms off the stage when the trail splits. I stand still. Inhale. And exhale. I nudge my GPS but it's still not talking to me. It's left. Definitely left. Left? Wait. What's that? Closer. Clooo-ser. Squint.

"Ho-ly shii-it."

A goat head. No body. Not even a neck. A fresh decapitated goat head rests on its chin, eyes stare down the left path, ears hang like extra-long velvet curtains. I tiptoe backwards.

"Okay. Right it is."

Within five minutes, a red/white waymark waves from a flat rock.

After hours of music and dancing, a raised red brick road slices across my path like a turntable needle across vinyl. The interlocking masonry looks powerful, yet lonely, begging me to follow it into parts unknown. Weeds reach over the edges like groupies. *If you build it, they will come.* Oops. Across the road, a painted red X forces a left-right decision. Left? Sure. My boots worship the smooth surface and speed-hike along. Through the green forest, the red road bends left and right, slopes up and down, like I've dropped into a *Perseverance* motivational poster.

It tosses me out to asphalt and a gruff-looking, stocky man—holding a shotgun.

"Uh, merhaba." I say and hold up my right hand, without a wave.

"Merhaba," says Shotgun Guy with a smile.

Who is he?

The town of Letoon starts out calm. Free-range chickens investigate under fruit trees in residential gardens. What's the penalty for stealing an orange? What if it's on the ground already? Solar panels balance on rooftops. Commercial greenhouses of tomato plants squish in-between houses. Shots fired! Shots fired! I stop and scan. Where's Shotgun Guy?

An outdoor rack stacked with potato chips signals a market.

"Welcome, welcome," a man says, "Merhaba."

"Merhaba."

I buy peanuts, potato chips, two tomatoes and a soft pretzel covered in sesame seeds. A woman adds two green peppers, no charge.

The clouds let go a downpour, and they both share concern about my t-shirt, which is already wet. I point to my rain jacket (it's too hot to wear) and show them more clothes in my backpack.

"*Pansiyon?*" he asks.

"No hotel, a tent, *çadir*," I say as I draw my triangle house on my hand.

"Oh," he says and whistles.

Shotgun Guy squeezes under the awning with us, a dead grey and turquoise bird in his hand.

"Yemek? For food?" and mime to eat.

"Evet," he says.

A cube van roars by with the roller door open at back. Inside cargo? The five Russian campers.

"Hey! Hellooo!" I yell and wave as they all point and wave back.

I skip by the Letoon ruins and follow the red/white waymarks painted on street poles to the town of Kumluova and its tea houses and shops. The extra stimuli of cars, crowds and clanging of dishes accelerate my fatigue.

"Hello, how old are you?" asks a young boy who runs up on the sidewalk.

"Forty-five, and you?"

"Eleven."

"Hello, what is your name?" asks a girl who runs up behind him.

"Michelle, and what is your name?"

"Sena."

"Do you learn English in school?"

"Yes. Bye!"

Boys on mopeds, too young by Canadian laws, zip by and shout, "Hellooo." Flat-bed trucks lug crates of tomatoes. Dolmuş drivers brake to ask if I need a ride.

"Yes," whisper my feet but I overrule, instead scanning hiding spots in the reeds along the river.

I scramble down the embankment, dump my pack and collapse, swallowed by the long grass. My pants instantly soak up water. I don't need to eat dinner. Or write. I can't peg the tent in the soft marsh, but I could just unroll it, crawl inside and zip it. An improvised bivy sack. The reeds lean in to tickle my ears. Steady traffic rumbles five feet behind my head. And the weight of my body displaces the water higher over my legs. I think it could work? I could be sleeping in seconds.

Wait, would Shotgun Guy mistake me for water fowl? I struggle to stand, glance at my watch (almost 4 o'clock) and walk.

An apple prevents a hunger-induced crash, and I cross the bridge which leads to the even busier town of Kinik—buses, cafés, markets, janitor supply stores, mechanic shops with dogs guarding out front. Where the hell is that statue? I ask five men working on a motorcycle. "Likya?" Two point across a field and up a hill. There? I reread my notes, *turn left at the Atatürk statue and follow sign to Xanthos.* Mustafa Kemal Atatürk, the Republic of Turkey's first president, led the country through independence in 1923, and a statue is in many town centres. I thank them but keep my same direction. With dwindling energy (read: cranky), I can't comprehend shortcut directions, I just need them to show me the route that matches the guidebook. I hear them say "Likya" and the rest is probably, *"Jeesh lady, trust us, it's right there."*

Winding through the city centre, ah, here's the statue, here's the sign for Xanthos. And, as my route arcs back, yes, there's that field, the shortcut. I pull myself up the steep hill the mechanics had pointed out and arrive at the Xanthos ruins. I give them a passing glance and keep moving.

"Likya?" I ask a man working in the trees.

"Likya," he says and points down the hill.

My tender feet balk but I backtrack down the hill and approach the security guard in the ruins office.

"Likya?"

"Yes, go up the hill and about 300 metres, go right," he says in perfect English.

Well, he sounds precise, confident. I trudge back up the hill and wave at the guy working in the trees. At about 300 metres, a rock balances on another in front of a field. Here? With my GPS not cooperating all day, the two rocks are all I got. I cross the field and although no waymarks appear, my map does show a trail near a road so I tuck into the trees to find a place to camp. By 5 o'clock I stand in a flat area surrounded by tent-camouflaging bushes, and drop my pack.

Easy route? No. Never did leave that 3D *Perseverance* poster. One final check of my GPS. It now works.

DAY 5

Xanthos to Üzümlü

AT 5:30, THE CALL TO PRAYER joins me in my dream and guides me out. No wind. No ants. No slant. I unzip the door, tie the fly back and squint in the sun. Me, sky and the birds have a lazy morning, a full hour of lolling.

I pack up and head across the fields. I had read that Turkish people love picnicking, but 7 o'clock on a Tuesday morning? I weave around blankets of multi-generational families as we exchange smiles and günaydins.

I run across a four lane highway and into an outdoor market being set-up. Clothing (all those floral pants). Blankets. Two-tier tea pots (say that six times). Toys. Meat. Peppers. Watermelon.

"Günaydin," I say to a young man at a clothing stall.

"Good morning," he says.

"You speak English?"

"A little."

"Is today a holiday?"

"Yes, May 19, a very important day for Turkish people."

One family hasn't set up yet and sits sidesaddle on a blanket drinking tea.

"Hoş geldiniz," a woman says as she waves me in without fanfare. We have food. You don't. Sit. Simple as that.

"*Hoş bulduk*," I say to complete the welcome greeting. "Teşekkür ederim."

Their shoes line up off the blanket so I set my pack in the grass and sit on my knees so my boots stay off the blanket too. The middle-aged woman, in floral pants, blue sweater vest and head scarf, rips a hunk of bread bigger than my hand and sets it in my lap. She hands me a hard-boiled egg which I peel. What do I do now? She smiles and uses a fork to mash the egg into the bread, then layers five slices of a white cheese on top. She slides over a plastic tub and I resist my urge to scoop into it like fine sand.

"*Tuz*," she says.

"Tuz, tuz," I repeat, "salt."

She adds a pinch and I add two more before she gently closes my culinary treasure chest. Their generosity silences me and I'm not sure I could speak more words even if I knew them.

"Çay?" asks a teenage girl.

"Evet *lütfen*, teşekkür ederim." Finally, I remember to use *please*.

She pours a glass of tea, adds a sugar cube and mimes to stir with the baby spoon. Four-and-five-year-olds crowd around and stare. One girl wears a t-shirt of Minnie Mouse in a floral head band, similar to her own.

"Ah, Minnie Mouse," I say and point to Minnie's head and then to hers.

"Minnie! Mouse!" yells a boy. The social ice obliterates and all the kids join in, giggling. "Hello hello hello! Minnie Mouse! Hello hello!" I slap my free hand over my mouth to stop any egg torpedoes as I laugh along.

A grandma with crossed arms eclipses the kids.

"Merhaba," I say.

"Hmmph. *Eş*?" she asks, frowning down on me.

A taxi driver at the airport had asked the same thing and taught me the word for spouse.

"Evet, Canada," I whisper as I lower my gaze. I usually wear a thin metal band on my ring finger. It helps when I want to deter unwanted male attention or when I want an easy explanation for travelling solo. But this trip, nothing but silver earrings. Not sure why I think the pierced holes in my ears will close after 35 years.

"Hmmph."

I want to flash my belly button ring but instead, flip both forearms over to hide my wrist tattoos and tug my pants even further over my ankles and boots. I'm relieved that I had tucked up my long hair under a baseball cap.

Motorcycles, mopeds and work trucks buzz along the road to Çavdir. I loop around the roundabout and follow the red/white waymarks down a road of houses covered in pink bougainvillea.

Ooo, a graveyard. Headstones from 1994 stand beside crumbling nameless, dateless slabs. Low tree limbs threaten to knock them all down but the hardy grass stands in front like bodyguards. No way am I camping anywhere near here tonight.

I lose the trail after the graveyard, so I bushwhack across the 45 degree slope of prickly scrub. Thank you for your help, poles. A road is below the mountain to my right, so I think I'm going in the right direction. GPS? Nope, won't even register a signal, although I keep trying. Three times, I hike straight up the mountain in attempt to cross the real path. The midday sun is powerful on the exposed mountain side and I feel my energy depleting. Fast. Here's one good thing about hiking solo: private meltdowns. Feel it? Let it out.

"Where's this fucking aqueduct?" I collapse on my bum, a distance not too far given the sharp angle of the slope, and lean into the shade of a single small tree. "Fuck off. Just fuck right off." I suck hard on my water spout. Nothing. I yank at the hot blue lifeline. Nothing. "F-uuuck. Stupid fucking thing." I drop my backpack in the brush, flip open the top compartment and pull up the top one-third of my water pack—no water. I yank it all the way out. Empty. "FUCK." I freefall backwards until prickles cradle my head. "Fuuuck." My panting slows to inhales and exhales as I follow the clouds across the sky.

Okay, I'm out of water. But I won't die. A road is down there and I could hitchhike to a town. I'm just hot. And lost. And I wanted to be in Akbel today. I know the more I fight, the more will show up to fight. I stare at the clouds for another 15 minutes. Okay, I'm back. I make a final 100 foot bushwhack straight up the steep slope, and there it is—the aqueduct. The hidden route seems so obvious once you're on it. Another minute and I pop onto a road next to a yard where two men work.

"Likya?" I ask and both point to a single-track trail across a field.

"Evet? Yes?" I ask.

"Evet."

"Evet?"

"Evet."

"Su var? There's water?"

"Evet," he says and holds up one finger.

One kilometre? One minute? One litre?

My feet don't want to leave the smooth road, but I want the trail. And I'm still pushing for Akbel.

About a kilometre from the road, a cement circle the size of a small car—a water cistern.

I remove the wooden slat lid. Darkness. Will my 50 feet of lightweight parachute cord be enough? I unclip my water bottle and tie the cord on with four half knots—the first knot when tying your shoelaces. Being my only bottle, I tie four more. *Really Michelle? Eight half knots? Do you think that's enough?*

Half knots are the only knots I know. My hiker friends had set up knot tying stations in their backyards—tarps, bear bags and hammocks. Others gave me knot tying books written for children. On a bus, a random survival guy demonstrated on bits of rope from his pocket (because survival guys always have bits of rope in their pockets). My dad taught me his butcher's knot. I practiced hundreds, only to arrive home and phone him within minutes: "Dad, I forgot." A real hiker/camper should know knots, right? I read, I watched, I studied, and I practiced. But it never stuck. Did I need the impressive when one all-purpose would do? I finally let it go and reverted back to the first knot I learned as a kid.

I lower the bottle about 20 feet. It lays flat on the water and then sinks as it fills up. I haul it up and it's clear—no obvious bugs or grit—and pour it into my water bladder bag. Six more plus two purifying tablets: success.

While waiting the 30 minutes for the purifying tablets to be effective, I prepare lunch. As I roll up tomato slices, long green peppers and cheese into a yufka, a couple from Germany walk up. We chat about how we came to be on the Lycian Way, our guidebooks and our routes (they're just doing a few day hikes).

"Do you want to walk alone or together?" he asks.

"I like walking alone, but I get lots of that so together for a bit is great," I say, "thanks for asking."

After a few hours of scouting for signs and comparing notes from our different guidebooks, we say goodbye when they stop to chat with another German couple at the aqueduct springs.

I continue along the dry stone of the aqueduct. The smooth surface creates a string of gratitude for the ease of walking. After crossing a small stream, the aqueduct now fills with a few inches of running water. What would life have been like thousands of years ago? I cross a gulley, then look back at my progress, but the trail is buried under scrub. How the hell did I just do that?

Boys playing at a waterfall point out the next way. The trail narrows and more scrub closes in. Thank you, pants.

Find the trail. Lose the trail. *Long route*, says my guidebook. I had been days ahead of schedule—it felt good to have banked extra time—but now I'm behind. Will I lose my Antalya hotel reservation? Miss my plane home? I have to get to Akbel.

A dirt road winds between houses but no trail. I go right in what I hope is towards Üzümlü but—woof-woof-woof-woof! I freeze as a gigantic beige dog charges down a driveway—my first Turkish Kangal. No tether holds him but he stops on his own, barking from the driveway's boundary.

The Kangal is a large sheepdog, but not so large that its speed or agility is affected. I had read they can run up to 50 km/h. Their sole purpose? Guard their sheep. Not herd them, guard them, protect them from wolves, bears and jackals, especially at night. While travelling, I hang out with street dogs, beach dogs, any dogs, but I had zero expectations of befriending a working Turkish Kangal.

As my blood flows again, I tiptoe backwards and retrace my steps to the dirt road, but it ends at a house. A tiny terrier barks from the safety of a balcony. A dead end at one end and a Kangal at the other. Now I just want to get to the next village of Üzümlü, forget the further village of Akbel. I return to the Kangal, now beyond his concrete driveway and blocking the dirt road. Do canine calming signals translate across continents? I turn sideways and take off my baseball cap. I exaggerate the signs that humans can do to calm a dog—fake a yawn and lick lip. Yaaawn and lick lick lick. He barks, turns around, looks once over his shoulder, barks twice more and retreats up his driveway. So you're just a little kitty cat, a little kedi, eh Kangal? But I decide to cut through the terraced yards anyways.

I crash through brush, pivot around trees and arrive at a rock wall at the back of a house. A villager sweeps below.

"Merhaba. Üzümlü?"

She points to her left, my right, without raising an eyebrow. I peer along the rock wall that parallels her driveway. It dead ends at bushes and at about seven feet high, too high for me to jump off.

I look back at her, "Evet?"

"Evet evet."

I guess I can drop my pack first? A seven foot drop still seems too high for my knees.

"Evet?" and I point again to the end of the wall.

"Evet evet evet," she says without looking.

I steady myself on the ten-inch wide wall. After shuffling a few steps, I look up to see steep stairs off the wall and to her driveway. How monumental the trust factor can feel from one perspective while appearing ridiculously silly from the other. I walk along her driveway to the road. The Kangal is now behind me, but he watches me until I turn the corner into Üzümlü.

First stop, a market for cold nectarine juice. The owner sets up a red plastic stool outside and I remove my pack first in fear of crushing the three spindles.

"Where are you from?"

"Canada."

"Likya Yolu?"

"Evet."

He holds up one finger.

"Evet."

He steps back and inhales quickly.

"Yep, just me."

At the Antalya bus station, the ticket guy had asked me if I was hiking alone. I had proudly said yes. Oh no, not good, very dangerous, he had said. I didn't need a non-hiking urbanite's opinion occupying my already fragile thoughts. Since, depending on who asks, I may say, "My friends are behind me," or simply, "I have friends." But right now, I need a pat on the back after my tough day, and his expression gives it to me.

A motorcyclist roars up and turns off the ignition. In comfortable silence, he shares a smoke with the market's owner. Black jeans tighten around muscular thighs as one leg stretches to the pavement while the other rests on the rear brake pedal. He unzips his slim cut leather jacket to reveal a tight grey t-shirt, no gut. With no helmet, I can admire his olive skin and green eyes.

"Merhaba."

"Merhaba, where you from?"

"Canada"

No smile, no chit chat. Tough silent type? No thanks. Beautiful to look at, but connecting over good conversation does it for me. Wait. I haven't seen a mirror in five days. Maybe it's the sweaty, stinky hiker garb and the pathetic kiddie chair squat in the dirt?

I thank the owner, fill up at the public taps and climb up the steep asphalt switchbacks. I want to camp. First place that works. Anything flat. Around the first bend—hey!—the German couple. They had stopped for a long slow lunch on a patio.

Twenty more minutes of up and we turn into the marked trail entrance. Within five minutes, olive grove terraces open up the view to the valley below, and the sea beyond that.

"Okay, that's it for me, I'll go to Akbel tomorrow."

I choose the lowest terrace, which looks like a green infinity pool and commence lounging. But I lie right on the thick grass this time, no sleeping pad. While car camping in Mexico, my ritual was to open a cold beer before setting up camp, but in Turkey, it's become earthing.

The full sun is perfect for laundry and charging solar panels. While my GPS never did work, trying it all day sunk the battery to 42 percent. I finally switched to my second pair of socks today as I think the soap, without a proper rinse, had irritated the sides of my feet. But I'm still wearing the same shirt, bra, underwear and pants, hand washing them as needed. Last chore? Chopping out the inner elastic cuffs of my pants, allowing the pant legs to roll up to mid-calf. A fair compromise, I think, between respecting Islamic dress codes and avoiding heatstroke.

No other hikers or villagers appear on the path, so for two hours, I write in solitude as the sun sets. At 8:04pm, I hear the call to prayer, and the deep voice bellows from a loud speaker at a mosque far below in the valley.

Time to stretch out. I check in with my body, and there are no complaints.

Scritch scritch scritch.

I track the sound, and a tortoise digs a hole under the rock wall.

"You silly tortoise, you're doing the hard route. It'd take you two minutes going over the top." I ponder picking him up but decide to leave him alone. He'll figure it out.

Later, as I lay in the darkness of my tent—scritch scritch scritch.

You made it. Silly tortoise.

DAY 6

Üzümlü to Gelemiş

EVERY MORNING, I PACK faster as things settle into their permanent places. The top section of my pack has become the kitchen—food, purifying tablets, Swiss Army Knife, combination fork-spoon. The lower zippered compartment, the bathroom—first aid kit, toilet paper, sunscreen, liquid soap, deodorant, tampons, toothbrush and floss. It's not just the weight of items that's critical, it's the number. It takes mental energy to keep track of them, pack them and search for, through and around them.

Today, I forgot to pack the tent poles. Usually I put them inside first, against one side of my pack and stuff everything around them. But instead of repacking, I slid them with my rolled up sleeping pad into the straps on the bottom of my pack. Perfection. As soon as I did it, I couldn't believe I used to pack them inside. How many other things do I do simply out of routine?

The red/white waymarks provide blatant guidance so my thoughts drift, mostly to Gabriola.

Fifteen months ago, the urge to sell my North Vancouver apartment, where I had lived for 15 years, got stronger. I had no boyfriend, no dog. Take my business on a cross-country road trip?

House sit around the world? Live in Antigua, Guatemala for a year? After the apartment sold unexpectedly, I chose to move temporarily near my dad, to be closer while he grieved his wife. I researched investment opportunities for the banked equity. "I've never gone wrong with buying land," said my dad.

Gabriola, a small island between West Vancouver and Nanaimo (on the larger Vancouver Island), is the same size as Manhattan but with only 4500 inhabitants. I first visited when I cycle-camped there 15 years ago. Having escaped the exorbitant rise in housing prices compared to Vancouver, Gabriola real estate was possible. The flexibility of my online business propelled the vacant lot idea into a permanent home idea. An island? I might get to live on an island? Four days before leaving for Turkey, I had put in an offer on a small yellow cabin. It was rejected. With the time crunch, I let it go without a counteroffer. But still I linger in the idea of living, working and writing in a tiny cabin on an island.

At Akbel, as I stop in at an outdoor fruit and vegetable market, the Beatles' "Eights Days a Week" whispers from a corner speaker. Oranges! Apples! Lettuce! I don't understand how so little can satisfy my hunger when I'm expending so many calories. As I sit on a rock under a tree eating a banana, a grey-haired man in a grey cap, great sweater, grey pants and grey shoes walks by, smelling a lone red flower.

"Merhaba."

"Merhaba," he says. "Bir?"

"Evet." I nod and smile. "Only me."

"Oya," and he walks away with a smile.

He doesn't realize, but I truly appreciate his positive feedback. Or maybe it's disbelief. Either way, it reaffirms that I am doing a bold adventure and reminds me not to minimize the significance to myself.

After a few hours trekking through pine and olive trees, I sit to eat an orange and read my trail notes: *a 2000-year-old engineering marvel at Delikkemer ... the water crossed the dry valley by means of a sealed siphonic pipe made of stone blocks ... each 90cm x 90cm, 50cm thick and with a 30cm diameter hole ... a large number are still in place but others have fallen from the wall and lie scattered in the lush grass.* I peek between my legs at the hole in my flat stone stool. I guess I'm here.

I follow under the aqueduct wall to the beginning of the Patara peninsula. The high elevation and exposed dirt road opens views to the sea's multi-depth blues. Navigation, easy. Gentle up and down, easy. But the sun is strong and direct.

After an hour, gentle feels challenging. Wait, how much water do I have? How much have I drunk? I change gulps to sips. Do I look? What if I look and there's hardly any? Fear. What if I look and there's lots? Relief. But what if there's none? Would knowing change what I can do right now? Is it better to not know?

My map shows two cisterns before Patara, but I don't know exactly where I am on the map. How will the cisterns be marked, if at all? Two fist-size rocks side-by-side on the side of the road pull my eyes even further left. Wait, is that a cement circle? I wade through the hundred feet of waist-high dry grass, clamber up, and peer through the darkness of the rectangular opening—water.

As I unload my purifying tablets, string and water bottle, two hikers appear on the road. "Merhaba, hello!"

Aiken and Laura are from England and hiking a few sections during their two week holiday.

"Is there a bucket?" he asks.

"I have an extra bottle."

"Ah, great, I don't think we brought enough water. Do you think it's okay?"

"I have extra purifying tablets."

Aiken hands me their lone one-and-a-half litre water bottle which I fill and plop in two tablets.

"Are you hiking alone?" asks Laura.

"Yes."

"Brave," she says. "Character building."

"Well, I'm better now, it's day six. A week ago I was terrified."

Challenging now feels gruelling, not from the steepness (although that doesn't let up), but the on and on. And on. I'm grateful for the non-stop sea view, therapy for my heat-induced crankiness. Turkish tall ships with clean, worry-free sunbathers on the decks provide contrast to self, but not a longing.

A dog barks once. There, up ahead to the left, a Turkish Kangal just off the road. Sheep on the right. A shepherd in-between. He holds up his palm and I stand still. Trust the shepherd. As he gets close to his dog, the dog lays down but doesn't break his stare at me. The shepherd rests his hand on the dog's neck and waves me on. I pass, silently, avoiding eye contact with the dog, the shepherd and the sheep.

Uphill, another hairpin turn, more uphill. My sips return to gulps. Tenderness in my soles deepens to burning, then searing. Shoulders slump, boots shuffle, as crankiness turns to dejection. I scout the land for campsites, and although I do have cheese and bread for dinner, and pears—pears!—for breakfast, camping doesn't feel right. Not here. Not yet.

A large red X painted on a rock next to the road questions my route. Which way then? A 360 degree scan reveals a tiny small white/red splotch of paint a few feet off the road to the right. The trail winds down, around, and in a few minutes I'm back standing on the same road, facing the same X. Huh? I try the red/white paint splotch trail again. And again, arrive back at the X. Well, this is bullshit. I check my GPS, it seems I'm on the trail. But where do

I go? Movement down the road nudges me from my trance. It's Eric and Gabby! It's Eric and Gabby, the day-hiking German couple!

"Oh am I happy to see you." I point to the X.

"Sometimes I think they're painted but not true," says Eric.

"That's a bit much on a tired brain," I say.

"Yes, true," he says. "But my GPS does show it's up this road."

I study his handheld GPS. The you-are-here triangle is like mine, but the detailed trail, sea, mountains, trees and roads are not like mine. We walk and chat about crime in Canada, Germany and Mexico, global warming and holidaying with children. We reach the highest point, and gravity leads us down. A Likya Yolu signpost indicates Patara, straight, or Kalkan, into the trees to the right.

"Okay, this is me."

"What? You're not going to see Patara?" asks Eric.

"No, I wasn't."

"Really? Oh but the beach is one of the longest in Turkey and the ruins aren't busy. It'd be a shame to come all this way and not see Patara," he says.

Do I share my apathy of organized ruin sites? *You're in a historically significant country and you're not going to visit ruins? What kind of traveller are you?* The beach could be incredible, though, maybe too incredible. *Ya, forget the hike. You deserve to lounge on a beach too.* I tag along to Gelemiş.

At the entrance to the town, Eric and Gabby find their pansiyon and we say goodbye. I continue to the village centre, maybe I'll buy food and hike back to the Likya Yolu? Or I can stop for the night. Stop? Stop.

"Pansiyon?" asks a man hunched in a cement stairwell, chubby flesh peeking between shirt buttons.

"No. Camping."

"What about camping on the roof?" Stairwell Guy says in English and points across the street.

"Hmm, can I see?"

I follow him through the pansiyon's courtyard, tables in one part set up with blue and white checked tablecloths but no dishes. The open kitchen is empty, at 5:30pm. We walk up three flights of crumbling concrete stairs to the roof. Mountains tower out front, but windows from neighbouring buildings look down on the roof from the other three sides.

"Showers?"

"In the rooms."

"How much for a room?"

"Thirty lira."

"Hmm. Fourteen bucks. Can I see?"

We go down one level and along an unlit hallway. The empty rooms have open doors, beds made. Is this pansiyon coming to life or waiting to die? He shows me a single room with a wobbly table-for-two and saggy bed. Lint and crumbs cover an area rug. I glance at Stairwell Guy, in plain dress shirt and scruffy beard. Does he even work here? I peek into the bathroom, the tiles look clean but a used condom coiled in the trash flings me backwards into his belly. A shower. A hot shower. A long hot shower. I have flip flops. I check the second door which opens to a long private balcony, overlooking the street.

"I'll take it."

He leaves and returns with a five gallon bucket of cold water, a one litre pail floating inside.

"The water isn't good, maybe in an hour."

Barter flashes across my mind. Other times, no problem. But exhaustion hushes my voice. And the thought of a shower (well, scooped water) dangles in front of me. I don't want to risk losing it. Other pansiyons, you ask? Doesn't even cross my mind. I'm not leaving. I'm 3.2 seconds away from getting wet. Getting wet, without camp clothes on. And five gallons? Opulence compared to three inches in a plastic bag. Plus, he's offered to fondle, er, machine-wash, my clothes.

"You can leave your clothes in a bin in the hallway."

"Okay thanks, thanks, yep, okay, got it, thanks, thanks a lot," and I close the door on his foot.

Inside lock? Broken. My pack dumped on the wobbly table and pushed up against the door substitutes nicely.

I'll spare you the shower scene. Let's just say the intensity of the ooo's and ahhh's of the rinse-wash-shave-shampoo-rinse could easily have been misconstrued.

I turn the tap of the freestanding sink to brush my teeth and water splashes my feet. No P-trap (or is that an S-trap?), only a six-inch pipe straight out of the bottom of the sink. The small rinse pail stands-in.

I shake the wrinkles out of my town clothes: black capri pants and lightweight merino wool V-neck. I wrap my pink scarf around my neck to complete the outfit and check charging levels of my phone and solar battery pack. Okay, everyone's happy.

I throw my hiking clothes into the blue plastic bin outside my room, bra and underwear tuck in the bottom.

"Fill yer boots, buddy."

Gelemiş is a tourist town with pale people in sun hats and markets displaying beach toys, sunscreen and halter tops. Outdoor cafes line the one main street, but because May is early in the season, they're mostly empty. I buy a new pen and miniature tube of olive oil-based face cream.

"Where shall I go for dinner?" I ask the English-speaking clerk.

"Osman's makes the best *pide*, right around the corner."

"Pide?"

"Oh, you haven't had pide yet?"

Osman's is empty. A man in chef's whites, including the towering white toque, welcomes me with a wave and shows me to a plastic table and chair on the patio, with a view of both the street and open kitchen. Clear rolled plastic replaces solid walls, and I use the salt shaker to keep journal pages from flipping back a week. I double up my scarf. Crazy hot, crazy cold.

I point to the photo of a pide covered in spinach. "*Ispanakli kasarli pide?*"

"Yes yes yes."

"*Bira?*"

He shakes his head. No alcohol.

"Coke?"

"Yes yes yes."

A cat sits on the stairs leading to a second floor. Another twirls around the legs of my chair. Kedi kedi kedi.

With a pen finally in hand, I download memory tidbits into my journal until he returns with food.

"Yes yes yes."

My shrieks scatter both cats. My left hand silences my mouth, lips trembling. My eyelids quiver in a bold attempt to hold back tears. Breath holds. I turn my head to shield my emotions from the open kitchen, but without language, maybe this is the best way to display gratitude. When was the last time he presented a meal that created actual tears? Straight from the wood-fire oven, the pinched edges of the crust droop over the plate. Melting white cheese wrestles with two, maybe three, cups of spinach across the oblong surface. One cut down the middle, six across. I wipe away my tears as I bend forward and breathe in. I scatter salt as if from a shotgun, twist free a slice and rest it on my tongue—one, two, three—before I tear into it.

Inspired by the three-word chef, I moan, "yum yum yum" plus low giggles before each and every, single, bite. The cats come back. After eating half, I am full. At home, I would have finished it. Easily. The appetite metamorphosis on long-distance hikes mystifies me.

I finish dinner and buy two cold Efes from the corner market.

"You want to party?" says Stairwell Guy as he points to my beer bottles. "Me and you?"

"No, I go to bed," I say. "My laundry?"

"On the roof," he says. "Good-night then."

"Teşekkür ederim, good-night."

I sit on my balcony, sip Efes and write, listening to the hum of the street. Conversations. Dogs barking. Mopeds. Construction. Finally at 8:04pm, the call to prayer—bedtime. After sunset, I snuggle into my sleeping bag and long for my tent and the goats.

DAY 7

Gelemiş to Kalkan

I INHALE MY LAVENDER-SCENTED white-again t-shirt as I hike up the hill to the Likya signpost for Kalkan. I'm all set with oranges, cucumbers and apples, two each, a heavier pack but it'll be worth it. Forget the beach, forget Patara.

The path is well-marked and easy around the peninsula and back to Delikkemer, so my mind wanders, first to my ex-boyfriend. Whoa, why's that coming up? It's been five years. I'm happy he's happy. Aren't I? Will my friends visit me on Gabriola? What should I call this book? Let it go, already. Just write.

Back at the Delikkemer-Patara junction, I stop to read my map and notes: *either walk to the main road and take a bus or continue to Kalkan on a narrow and dramatic cliff path along steep rocks. If you use the cliff path, send your rucksack ahead by bus, as this path involves scrambling and is difficult with a full pack.* Send ahead by bus? How?

A young man on a moped rides up and idles by the Likya Yolu signpost.

"Akbel," he shouts and points left. "Patara," and points right.

"Kalkan?"

He hops off his moped and floats down the embankment. He studies my map, standing close enough that our hips touch. Then:

our heads snap up like pairs skaters. I swat his hand away from the tight grip on my ass. Our eyes meet. Did-that-just-happen? I-am-in-the-middle-of-nowhere-by-myself. He-is-bigger-than-me. This-is-not-okay. What-if-he-hits-me-back? I-don't-care. This-is-why-many-women-don't-travel-on-their-own. You-so-picked-the-wrong-fucking-woman.

"Fuuuck. Youuu," I whisper, inches from his face.

My knees bend as my body twists left, my left hand cups my right and propels it backwards until my right elbow explodes into his chest. He recoils.

"Fuuuck youuu!" I yell.

He scrambles up the hill on all fours, causing a landslide and dirt bomb.

"Fuck you, fuck you! Fucking coward!" I scream as both middle fingers pump into the air. "You stupid, fucking idiot!"

He throws a leg over his moped and scurries away with the rear tire tucked so low underneath, the taillight illuminates his asshole.

My right hand karate chops my left elbow, the reflex thrusts my left fist into the air. Again and again.

"Yeah, you fuck, fuck, right, offffff!"

I shimmy my pack off just as he u-turns.

"Oh yeah? You wanna fuck with me? You picked the wrong fucking woman!" I yell as I dry hump the air between us. "Fuck youuuuuu!"

His engine revs high as he passes me, but fades out on the long, straight stretch of dirt road, until he disappears.

I look over both shoulders. Alone and in silence, my adrenaline freefalls.

"Too much?"

I snort. Giggles increase to belly laughs, which reverberate down the mountain as I fall to the ground, my hands trampolining off my stomach. I only stop laughing when my abdominal muscles cramp into a solid mass, halting oxygen.

"Well, he won't do that again."

I lay flat on my back and mix tears with face dirt. Then I pick myself up, lift my pack and walk towards Kalkan. For the next while, as I follow the easy trail, I muse about my strong reaction to the ass-grab. It's not the first time.

When I was 19, I lived in a high-rise apartment in the West End neighbourhood of Vancouver. One night, I was a half-block from home when a guy came from behind and grabbed my shoulder and ass. I spun around and punched him in the face with an open palm. He ran away into the darkness of the alley.

A few years later, I was on the SkyTrain (Vancouver's rapid transit system), in a car with six or seven strangers. A drunk man got on and reached out to grab me as he sat down. "You're   (hic) pretty," he mumbled.

I slid out from under him, turned and punched him in the chest, twice.

"Get the fuck, off of me, asshole," I said and moved to a seat opposite him.

"But I think you're (hic) pretty."

He stood up and leaned forward to sit next to me again but fell into me instead. I slithered out from under him, stood up and shoved him backwards. He collapsed in a lump. At the next stop, I yelled for the station attendant, "This guy's totally drunk and keeps grabbing me. He needs to go." No one else on the train said or did anything—to me, to the drunk or to the attendant.

When I was 33, I was running to work through Vancouver's 1000-acre Stanley Park. As I ran over the pedestrian bridge, a man was facing the bushes but looking over his shoulders. Both hands clutched his groin. Urinating? He turned, stared at me, and stroked his penis, fast. Here was that moment. That moment that keeps so many women from walking in the park, alone.

"Oh man, are you kidding me?" I said and stood still, panting. "You stupid asshole, feels good, doesn't it?"

He kept doing it, even faster.

"Come here."

He slowed. Stopped.

"Come here."

He zipped his pants. Stood motionless at first, then walked away.

I walked towards him.

He looked over his shoulder and walked faster.

"Stop, I'm a Vancouver police officer! Stop!"

He ran down a trail, with me in pursuit. I picked up a three-foot long stick and again yelled, "Vancouver Police, stop, you're under arrest." He kept running.

After five minutes, he was slowing, I was gaining, so he stopped and turned. Fight time?

"Si-iiit d-owwwn!"

He sat. After catching my breath, I marched him out of the park and from a payphone, I called 911 for other officers to assist.

"Oh fuck yeah!" I say and jump to high-five a tall scrub branch. I'm all fired up when two women from Holland appear on the path.

"How's the trail up ahead?" I ask.

"It's tricky," says one.

"But you'll do it," says the other.

A moment later, I'm here. I stand at the bare rocks, on the edges of the rounded cliff, expansive sea below and beyond. I've read ahead in the notes. More tricky trail segments are coming. I need perspective. I need to know what *narrow, dramatic cliff path* means. I need to know how difficult is *difficult*.

But where do I go? The rocky slope disappears over a curve like a convex mirror. I stretch over further, and the rocks have jagged outlines as if partially put through a paper shredder. I collapse my poles and cinch them to my pack. These are boulders, boulders the size of people—some standing, some crouching.

The faded red/white waymark, on the last rock before the curve ends, signals: *Over here! Over here!*

"But, that's the edge," I whisper.

I grab the first sharp rock. I need to move facing forwards so I can search for waymarks and hand holds. But I feel about as safe as climbing down a ladder facing forwards. The waymarks move away at the same pace I move towards them. I apologize to the stone people for bashing into them, still unsure of my wide load. The three-point anchor rule inches me forward: hand-hand-foot or foot-foot-hand.

Slower.

The shreds grip my hands back (good) and also my soles (bad). Two hands plant forward on separate rocks and want a foot to join them, but the rock behind grips my foot and won't let go. The delay of my foot placement propels my weighted body forward towards the sea. My heart rate surges just as my foot snaps free and slams into its rightful place.

Breathe.

As I reach each waymark, I scan for the next, and another cliff edge pulls me in. *Ya, come to the cliff edge, a little bit further, a liii-ttle bit further, aaand, okay-go-left.*

Over and over.

Focus.

My eyes snap up and take in a gulley and another climb. With my mind traversing over there, a left hand and a right foot drop together over a boulder. But the rolled sleeping pad on my pack's bottom makes contact, bounces me off and propels me forwards. "Shit shit shit." My left foot dives forwards and pins against a rock.

As I stand still and breathe, I glance across the gulley again and see four dots of colour bouncing towards me. Okay, that's where the trail goes. That flash of the future calms me.

But now, I'm stuck. I can't go down. I can't go back up. Will I splash straight in or snag on the rocks like a kite? How quickly can I unclip my pack before I sink?

Foot. Hand. Foot.

Sideways? Sideways keeps me on the path, but sideways pulls out my triangle anchor.

Move.

I dig in hard with my left hand and left foot for the two-point anchor. I lean out to the sea and swing my right arm and leg out and across to the left until momentum turns me, slapping me into the next rock. I wrap my arms and legs around it, lingering in my victory of rock-paper-scissors.

Too much wobble. I need to ground.

"I can't believe you're doing this with a huge pack," say the four colourful dots, aka four British men.

"I'm doing it!"

"Well, you've only got a half-hour more."

As I land on solid dirt, my pain monitoring system switches on again and my feet remind me of their tender souls. After the intensity, my brain needs a time out to refuel. Leftover pide! I rest and nibble pide as I watch Kalkan's white, three-story villas clutch the cliffs in the distance. I know the feeling.

I walk by triple infinity pools in homes with brass gate plaques engraved with names like *Villa Clara* and *Villa Blue*. Drills and hammers echo from construction sites. At patio cafés, chalk yells cocktail specials for 13 lira. Women in sundresses clink wine glasses with grey-haired men in linen. Do I still have dirt on my face?

A chubby dog on the sidewalk trips me. He opens one eye from his nap and rolls onto his back, inviting a tummy rub. I bend to accommodate.

I stop to buy a large bottle of water and take pleasure in a can of nectarine juice as the central square buzzes. Rented scooters park ten-deep. Trucks deliver flats of bottled water to convenience stores. Tour guides bark out offers. Sunburned drunk guys zigzag through traffic as pony-tailed girls in bikini tops, mini skirts and platform flip flops try to keep up. Once the juice is gone, so am I.

I wind through the narrow alleys lined with clothing and jewellery shops and end up at the divided highway. I mime-ask a local woman if I can walk on the highway with my wide pack, but I am unclear if her head shake is the answer or incomprehension. The desire to be in my tent compels me up to the highway just as a dolmuş pulls over and blocks me.

"Ulugöl?" asks the driver, indicating the next town.

"Evet, *ne kadar*?"

He holds up two fingers.

I climb in and sit on the small forward seat near the driver, giving him two lira from my cargo pocket.

"Likya?" he asks.

"Evet."

Within a few minutes, he drops me off at a Likya Yolu signpost and I dart across the two-lane highway. The trail squirts up between two houses before levelling on olive terraces. Stop or keep going to Bezirgan? The clouds now touch the olive trees. Rain falls. I venture 50 feet off the trail, a flat spot under a tree looks right. I skip my earthing ritual, set up my tent and crawl inside to escape the chill.

As I sit in my tent, rain bounces off the nylon and my eyes get moist. My head slumps, the top brushes against my bra suspended from the ceiling. My hands flop palms up between my open, outstretched legs.

Nobody would see me if they walk the trail, but they would hear me. But for the next 20 minutes, I don't care. I can't stop the tears.

And the need to question the tears is strong. But do I need to know?

I like wine on patios too. So why did I rush through Kalkan? Too much stimuli after the trail silence? Sure. But what else?

I'm a strong woman, I can do it. I can hike in the rain and fog by myself. But making all the decisions is hard.

Keep going.

I don't have my dog yet. I don't even have a home. I'm all by myself. I've been by myself for five years. I'm a good, loving person. I'm a happy person. I meet people. I'm so open to meeting a nice man and sharing a home, a dog, a life. So where is he?

Fuck. I'm crying about men?

Self-ridicule tries to sneak in, but instead I manage to practice a morsel of self-compassion. *It's okay to feel loneliness. And it's okay to want a grey-haired man in linen too.*

I stuff headphones into my ears. Waterboys. Moby. Beatles. Cat Power. It works. I write for two hours and fall asleep before the evening call to prayer.

DAY 8

Kalkan to Bezirgan

T HE ACOUSTICS OF HARD RAIN on stretched nylon soothes me. With closed eyes, I tap the four corners of my tent and under the zipped door. Dry. I flop back and submerge my head under my sleeping bag. This freestanding MSR Hubba NX solo backpacking tent, with its side vestibule and door, aluminum poles and less than three-pound total weight, is my dream tent. Although I could do without the dark, head-size lettered logo pressed on the side, which on more than one occasion, has looked like a person (or monster) peeking in as though through a tinted car window.

I slip on Defeet Woolie Boolie merino wool cycling socks, first bought 15 years ago for cycle commuting to the police department during Vancouver's rainy winters. A blind date with my hiking boots proved successful, and they've been inseparable ever since. Warm when cool, cool when warm and no blisters. Ever. Plus a cartoon sheep on the bottom of each sock brings a welcome smile on tough days.

Do I have to go? Is it foolish to wander off into the mountains in a monsoon? I've already broken two classic rules: not telling anyone my planned route and no hiking buddy. I'll be adding the likelihood of wet clothes and no stove or ability to build a fire. But my notes say it's only four-and-a-half hours. I whip off the fly, shove it into a plastic bag and stuff the tent into its stuff sack. I slip on my waterproof jacket and start walking.

No goat bells, no birds, no bugs, no people and, due to the fog, no perspective on where I'm going or how far I've come. Not even the clacking of my poles. Instead, they slip off saturated tree roots. My black jacket transforms from matte to gloss as I wind through farm fields.

I climb into a small village, where rain slaloms the stone road, providing the only movement in the streets. A fork in the road stumps me, and I contemplate as raindrops cliff-dive of my hood brim and splash over my eyeballs. Left for the switchbacks? Or right, for the warmth, companionship and tea in the village market? Left or right?

"*Sol!*" yells a voice.

Left it is then.

"Teşekkür ederim!" I yell and wave to dark windows behind me.

Up, up, turn. The trail is well-marked, and I don't have to disturb my GPS, not once. With no animals present to counterbalance rising fear, I sing. But without printed lyrics I don't get beyond a line or two for each song. An improvised Beatles' "Eight Days a Week" seems to stick:

"I'm hiii-king up the Tuuurk-ish mooountains... eiiight days a weee-eeek!"

"Liiik-yaaa." (splash splash) "Yooo-luuu." (splash splash)

The pools of water around flat rocks demand twisty dance steps as I keep pace with the (splash splash) chorus.

There is only one distinct path up the switchbacks, and I'm grateful that the creepy-foggy-monsoon is not also creepy-foggy-monsoon-plus-no-waymarks.

The singing halts as thoughts of Days 19, 27 and 28 sneak in. *Mobile phone will not work... the mountains are totally deserted... don't walk mountain sections alone... sudden heavy rain and thunderstorms ... you have to carry enough supplies to last several days ... you require experience of GPS use and map- and compass-reading skills ... the path is sometimes difficult to find ... water is scarce and unreliable.* Totally deserted. Don't walk alone. The whole trail has felt isolated. I rarely see anyone on the trail, only in the villages. I walk through a village everyday, but the last three days? No anonymous voices shouting out directions. Can I carry three days worth of food? Will the sun have dried up all the water sources? Three litres of water for three days? No way. I don't want to do it. I don't think I can do it—a rock the size of my head slices through the switchbacks and disappears into the fog. My heart attempts to give chase but is held back by the wiser, stronger sternum.

"Uh, hellooo?"

You'd think I'd be relaxed about things going bump in the dark after policing for nine years. But it's a primal, base fear. I remember a missing persons incident involving an apartment search. Usually, it was fun to peer around peoples' homes in their absence but not that place. My patrol partner and I weaved around life-sized sad clowns, Greek statues, naked headless dolls, knights holding swords and corseted manikins, until we were stopped by a red velvet couch—and a pair of human feet resting on the couch's arm. Sleeping? Were we too late? As we slinked around the couch in opposite directions, the body snapped his eyes open and said "Boo!" Although I didn't scream, I jumped back, despite cement-like patrol boots and a twenty pound duty belt. I'm sure I became his forever party joke. "Oh yeah? Well get this, one time I scared this cop..."

The switchbacks will lead me directly to the source of the sound. There are bears in Turkey, but not in this area.

Well, it ain't no tortoise.

It turns out, it's only waterlogged earth not able to contain itself.

I finally reach the plateau, but the promised view is absent due to lingering and thickening fog. Wind flicks my bare hands. I pull my hood strings tighter, producing tunnel vision. My body shivers as I schlep downhill.

"Eight days a week...."

This no longer appeases. I go quiet.

Hey look, a dozen huts on stilts, each with a number above the troll-height doors. Goat motel? Grain storage? Under the last one, goats take cover and hover, butts out.

"Smart, I might be joining you."

Asphalt. *Turn east*, say my notes. It feels like I should go right. Is right, east? As I dig for my compass, the fog lifts enough to reveal a red painted X on a street pole to the left. Okay, definitely not left. But above the X, in the fog's shadow, another sign— *Pansiyon* ← *500m*. I go right in search of a campsite.

A man in knee-high rubber boots smokes a cigarette under an umbrella in front of his house.

"Merhaba," I mumble, with a half-smile, one that he can't see because of my improvised balaclava.

"Awww, merhaba," he whispers back.

Two women in a field use single hands to hold rebellious clear plastic sheets over their heads. The other hands work long-handled tools.

"Merhaba," I whisper without waving when they glance up.

I attempt perspective. They have to work in this downpour. It's their livelihood. I'm choosing to be here. It's my holiday. I shouldn't feel sorry for myself—but I still can't keep my head from hanging. I no longer walk around puddles. Both poles drag, straps looped around one wrist. A few newly painted cement houses stand amongst old stone houses with padlocks on front doors and gates, some with wooden shutters nailed shut, others swollen beyond their frames. Water bombards my body from all sides as I pass the water taps. Was it only two days ago I was scared by scarcity? A public bathroom. A mosque. A yellow Likya sign points to the next town. No. Tomorrow. Tonight I'll stay here, in Bezirgan.

In the closet-size market, a man sits in the dark amongst packaged goods.

"Merhaba, pansiyon?" I ask. I've decided.

He points across the street.

"Pansiyon? Evet?" I ask again to confirm.

He gives directions in rapid-fire Turkish. I simply nod and say thank you. Two men sit in an alcove next door.

"Pansiyon?" I ask.

One man points down a street and my feet pursue the possibility, no longer connected to my head. I walk. I shiver. For 35 more minutes I walk through deserted farmland. Wait. Am I doing a big circle back to that pansiyon sign?

A man in rubber boots and umbrella approaches to shake my hand, "Merhaba."

"Merhaba, pansiyon?"

He mimes a left turn coming up. I don't want to leave his shelter, but I have nothing left to say. With an elusive pansiyon, I again consider camping ideas. What if I break in? That one, the one with the wonky shutters? No? The covered area under the stilts? What about that back porch? Back at the mosque?

Ahead, a wooden board is nailed to a street pole—*Owlsland.* A pansiyon? I follow the sign for five minutes and come upon a little house with a late-model pick-up truck out front. Is it a bed and breakfast? Somebody's private home? Either way, I need help. Pink and yellow flowers in the garden entice me through the gate just as a man comes out of the house.

"Merhaba, pansiyon?"

"No, it's a little further. I can drive you," he says.

I glance at my puddle, pooling outward from my feet like a lethal wound, "Oh, that's kind but not necessary, thank you. Is it far?" I say.

"No, only 100 metres, next right."

"Thank you then, I can walk."

The next house has the sign—*Owlsland.* I push open the gate and it clangs when my numb fingers slip off the cold metal. The path through the country-style garden leads to the separate garage, where two dogs lay on the ground and another two share a round bed. None bark. *Sod the dog, beware the owner*, reads the sign above. I like her already. Another dog on the house's front doorstep rolls over.

"Oh hello beautiful. I can definitely scratch that belly of yours."

After priorities, I strike the brass knocker and a Scottish woman answers.

"Hello, wow, what a day to walk," she says.

"Yeah, it's quite something," I say. "Do you have a room?"

"Yes, let me get my boots."

Pauline married her Turkish husband Erol, and for 16 years they've lived in Bezirgan, where Erol was born. Together, we walk around almond and fig trees, through another gate, along a grass field and stop at a freestanding building. She opens the door directly into a bedroom—"... and there's a hot shower, kettle for tea and a hair dryer..." My eyes moisten. Heat? Hair dryer? Tea?

"Oh my, I think I'm going to cry," I say as my hands slap over my mouth to hide the quiver.

"Well, don't do that, we have enough water for today," she says. "We usually do dinner at 7 o'clock, unless you'd like earlier?"

"That's fine. Any chance of a vegetarian version?"

"Yes, no problem."

The dogs run around the fenced yard that attaches to this small farmhouse. Pauline tells me this original farmhouse is 150 years old and has been in Erol's family for that long. She leaves me in the room where I stand motionless to absorb the extravagance: stone floors, white washed walls, thick dark wood beams and a fireplace with a crooked wooden mantel. Metal lanterns hang from the ceiling and wooden hooks carved from tree limbs adorn the walls. I turn on the wall heater with the remote control and set it at 26 degrees Celsius. I peel off my clothes and replace them with a fluffy white bath towel. I open the shower door, but movement inside makes me recoil and slam back into the sink, my towel slumping to the floor.

Scorpion.

I grab my hiking boot and poke at it—its tail curls. Call Pauline? No phone. Put wet clothes back on and tramp over to her house? No way.

I swing my boot like a lumberjack and wipe up the splayed body parts with a handful of toilet paper.

"So sorry little buddy but this hot shower is happening right freakin' now."

Goosebumps shrink in the tropical heat. I hand wash my laundry, and the wooden hooks are perfect for drying. With Pauline's permission, I string up my damp tent from nails poking from the beams. Outside, my tent fly hangs under the covered deck. I unroll my sleeping pad and hang up my backpack on the last empty wall hook. I plug in my solar battery, phone and MP3 player—and the kettle. Shall I have lemon or *böğürtlen*, which according to the photo on the teabag, is blackberry. Lemon or blackberry? Both! I unwrap the last of my cheese and create an appetizer plate with roasted peanuts and chocolate chip cookies. I bury my body under the bed's heavy blankets and nibble in the dark. It's only 2 o'clock and I have nothing I must do and nowhere I must be. Heat, tea, snacks and non-rationing electricity. I crank music. I write. I study maps. I roll around in my blanket fort.

I return to the main house for dinner: lentil soup and bread to start, a potato, eggplant and carrot stew, a green apple and cucumber salad, plus another green salad with yogurt dressing. The dessert is mint tea and biscuits.

"I thought you'd be starving," says Pauline, clearing serving platters still half-full of food. "It's weird. You'd think so, but I seem to fill up fast."

Pauline tells me about Kalkan Association for the Protection of Street Animals, the local organization where she volunteers. KAPSA runs a weekly winter feeding program where volunteers give donated food to other volunteers who then feed their local street dogs in 48 mountain villages. Their trap, neuter, return program, with a primary goal of no more puppies, is a success. Three thousand animals have been spayed or neutered since 2008, when KAPSA was formed.

"A lot of people say that they should do this and they should do that, but who is this they?" she says, "If everyone did just a little bit."

As I sip mint tea, I cuddle with Daisy, a shepherd mix, and with Dolly, a smaller shepherd with one blue eye and one brown eye.

At evening's end, Pauline offers to dry my hiking boots on her heater, and I tiptoe back to my farmhouse in her blue ballerina flats.

DAY 9

Bezirgan to Ufkadere

I WAVE GOODBYE TO THE farmhouse, and sunbeams guide me to Pauline's patio where Daisy airmails a woof from her doorstep. "Günaydin, Daisy, enjoy your nap."

"Puppy puppy puppy!" I coo to the four-legged butt-wiggler who weaves around my calves.

On the outdoor table, crystal and china rest upon the white linen, along with muesli and yogurt, fresh bread with three choices of jam, hard-boiled eggs, three kinds of cheese and local honey plus yellow and pink flowers. My appetite is not yet awake, but I sample everything as Pauline and I continue our conversation about dogs.

"What else am I going to spend my money on? There's no cinema or theatre. Makeup? Clothes? Wellies are enough. I have no kids. I'll leave my money to the dogs," she says. "As my grandmother says, there are no pockets in a shroud."

I could listen to her for days, but clouds darken. Daisy moves inside.

"Thank you for the conversation and lovely stay," I tell her. "I'm so grateful for Owlsland, for you, and for all you do for dogs."

She stuffs two plastic bags into my still-wet boots and hugs me goodbye, slipping an orange into my hand.

I follow Pauline's directions for a short cut to the village. At the bus stop, a man in a beige suit tells me he works in tourism in Kalkan.

"When does the market open?" I ask.

"He'll come in 15 minutes."

I look into the grey clouds and again at my watch. A white Mercedes pulls up and Suit Guy jumps into the backseat.

"Kalkan?" he asks me, before shutting the door.

"Um. No, I think I'll walk, but thank you."

A vintage turquoise motorcycle roars up, rider bouncing on the saddle seat, and parks underneath the shutters of the market. I buy cheese, peanuts, chocolate cookies and a loaf of bread, which I rip into two and squeeze into my kitchen compartment. Soggy bread sucks. I pull on my waterproof jacket and shuffle towards the Likya Yolu signpost pointing to Saribelen.

Within minutes, it's raining harder than yesterday. I stop and look back at the bus stop. I walk backwards—toe-heel, toe-heel—but pause, then spin around.

"Mountains it is."

But, pause yet again. I check my map. Saribelen is smaller than Bezirgan. Would a pansiyon even be an option?

"Dolmuş? Saribelen?" I ask a man back at the bus stop.

"Evet" he says and nods with a big smile.

"Dolmuş Gökçeören?"

"Hayır," Smiley Guy says and shakes his head.

"Dolmuş Kaş?"

"Evet," says the next guy, nodding, as he twirls a bag of fresh bread.

"Kalkan?"

"Evet," says Bread Guy.

I don't want yes and no answers. I want them to tell me what to do. If I take a bus to Saribelen, I'll only trim off a few kilometres, but if it's still raining the next day? Bypass Saribelen completely and walk the 14-kilometre road to Gökçeören? Wait here for better weather? But I don't have extra days, nor do I have a budget to stay a second night at Owlsland. If I take a bus back to Kalkan, then what? A bus to Kaş? That shortens the Likya Yolu by two days. That feels like cheating. But, I used to think that running a marathon was only official if you ran every single minute of it, no walking. Then I trained for my first 50-kilometre race, walked a lot and yet crossed the finish line feeling every bit worthy of the finisher's medal. Is this about walking every inch of the trail or about the adventure overall?

But I still want Smiley Guy or Bread Guy to give me permission to take the bus.

I point to my watch. "Dolmuş, Kalkan?"

The third and last man, a silent elder, untangles his hands from his sweater and points to the ten on my watch before staring ahead again. Smiley Guy nods.

Forty-five minutes to make a decision. In the meantime, I get private language lessons with three tutors.

A dolmuş pulls up and a hiker jumps out—Peter from Germany. Why do I expect every German to know English? Through mime and maps, I learn he's hiking the whole route, staying in pansiyons and has just bussed in from Kalkan. I mime that as far as I understand, there isn't a dolmuş going east from here, only back to Kalkan first, then eastward to Kaş. He shrugs his shoulders and laughs at his crumbling plan as he rubs and blows on his hands.

"Yep, cold here, it's not like the coast."

Peter takes a photo of me and the Turkish men, and when I share it, Silent Elder smiles for the first time.

Forty minutes later, the dolmuş arrives and we stuff our packs in and climb aboard. We pass through tiny Saribelen, and the rain continues to pour. Yesterday's four hour hiking route condenses to 20 minutes, and we arrive back in Kalkan. Together, we walk down to the highway and flag over another dolmuş, full of English and German tourists. We both strike up conversations in our native languages.

"You're hiking the Lycian Way, yet you are on a bus?" asks one Englishman.

"Yeah, uh, I already had that conversation with myself," I say.

The half-hour ride to Kaş is along a two-lane highway, with steep stairways to teeny coves on the right and abrupt, dusty mountain walls on the left. The driver navigates the twisty road with one hand spinning the steering wheel and the other holding a cell phone to his ear. Clouds stay but rain goes.

The Kaş bus station is right on the Lycian Way, and Peter and I say goodbye. He's going to stay the night. Restaurants with rolled up walls are next to restaurants with patios, and those are next to restaurants with views. All are open for business but not yet filled with tourists. Climbing vines frame narrow, three-story hotels. Rental signs hang in apartment windows above jewellery shops. Dogs lounge in the main square, except one shepherd who plays with a deflated red ball.

How much is rent here? Could I get a three-month summer rental after my hike? If I buy a laptop, I could run my business from here.

After a few more streets, the cafés and hotels end and single dwellings start. A few more minutes beyond that, the coastal road leaves town for good. I pull out tomorrow's map and glance at the heading without reading the notes—two more hours to Liman Ağizi.

The cracked asphalt curves right onto a dirt road which eventually dissolves into red muck, my boots stamping like a wax seal. The imprints deepen.

"It's like dog shit. It's like dog shit covered in olive oil. It's like dog shit, covered in olive oil and slush. It's like dog shit, covered in olive oil and slush and licked by a dinosaur."

A grass field ends the silliness, and I move smoothly across, go left, and cross back into scrubs and trees. Did I miss Liman Ağizi?

I read my notes: did I miss the *house with turrets* or not yet? Was that farm back there the *isolated farm*? Was that the wall for the *circle behind the buildings to a field wall and turn left with the wall on the right*?

I read more: *don't do this route alone, in wet weather or with a large pack*. Shit. No, not dog shit. Just shit shit.

I read further for the Liman Ağizi to Boğazcik route: *a wild, long and often difficult route and the cisterns are not dependable in summer, take plenty of water*.

GPS shows I'm on the trail. But am I before Liman Ağizi or after?

My chest tightens and I breathe slower in attempt to release it.

Go back? No. I despise backtracking.

Water? Check. Food? Check. Daylight? Check. I move forward.

I follow the waymarks and dead-end at a stack of boulders, and beyond, a cliff. A ledge 30 feet long hangs off the rock like a slim, picture frame shelf. Um, with dinosaur spit on my soles? I unclip my pack, squeeze my shoulder blades together and let it crash. I peek over the drop-off. The sea slam dunks waves ten feet up the vertical rock.

"This is bullshit."

I adore the sea. I need the sea. But to be near it or on it, not in it.

Like many, it probably started in 1979 when I saw *Jaws* as a ten-year-old, and despite opportunities to overcome it, it never went away.

"To kayak solo, you'll first have to demonstrate a roll," said the instructor. "Well, that's never going to happen," I said, committing to kayak partners, forever.

When I toured Titanic Belfast (a museum where the ship was built), I was both fascinated and freaked by the re-enactments. People trapped in sinking ships? Nightmares. People trapped in sinking ships and leaving their one tiny air pocket to swim into the unknown in search of another tiny air pocket? Total insomnia.

In the late 90s, I signed up for scuba diving lessons. The pool session? Giggled through that. Ocean dive? As I anchored myself 30 feet below the surface, my body refused to cooperate for the mandatory assignment—simply taking the regulator out of my mouth. I took the fail.

The dirt erodes between my pack and the drop-off as I pace. Should I wait for others? According to the heartbeat hypothesis, I'll be wasting precious finite beats waiting in this accelerated state for rarely-seen hikers.

I collapse my poles, pull my pack on extra tight and haul myself up the first boulder. Wait, a foot path? My elevated vision reveals a narrow foot path, a really narrow foot path, but it's not on the bullshit scale. That thin ledge? It hangs above the trail, useful for hand holds.

I scramble rock-to-rock along the deserted coastline and after hours, a building appears across the bay.

"Merhaba! Hello!" a voice echoes across the water.

I meet one brother who introduces me to the other, both fluent in English. They bought the investment property 14 years ago and have since built a restaurant, a patio lounge plus camping terraces and a few rooms to rent. Over 300 of their olive trees fill the space between the restaurant and a two bedroom house up the hill.

"Do you have showers?" I ask.

"Yes, and will you need help with that?" a brother asks with a wink.

"Oh, you'll be the first to know if I need help soaping up," I say with a wink back. Nine years working in a male-dominated police department taught me how to play the game.

After setting up camp and taking a shower, I find the only other traveller on the patio. Ibrahim is Turkish, tall, lanky, and writes in a notebook as his feet rest on a chair. He doesn't speak English so I share my list of Turkish words and Google Translate app. We connect instantly, and teach, learn, laugh, and create inside jokes for the next two hours.

"Is the tall guy gone, Michelle?" asks a brother.

"For now," I say, as my eyes follow Ibrahim walking to his campsite of just a blanket and a small pack.

The other brother prepares a vegetable stew, rice and salad for dinner, and Ibrahim returns, along with two fishermen.

After dinner, the setting sun reduces the light on the open patio and the fishermen build a fire. Pen in hand, I sit in a club chair in front of it, my journal balancing on my crossed legs and an Efes bottle wedged between my thigh and the leather.

At a four-person card table, the brothers and fishermen play *okey*, a tile-based game. *Click*—the confident player lays a plastic tile. *Clack*—the losing player slams a tile which ricochets off another and propels it to the floor.

"Hey Michelle, come play!" says one brother.

"Hey Michelle, I need a cheering section!" says the other brother.

I peek at Ibrahim, who looks up from a Turkish translation of *Incognito: The Secret Lives of the Brain*, by neuroscientist David Eagleman, and roll my eyes. He rolls his eyes too. We share smiles.

"Hey Michelle, are you writing your life story over there or what?" says one brother.

My forehead crinkles, and my ally creates a mirror-image of my disdain.

"Hey Michelle, I need a good luck kiss," says the other brother.

Ibrahim continues to read about mindfulness, while I continue to write about Ibrahim reading about mindfulness.

DAY 10

Ufkadere to Boğazcik

I HAD FALLEN ASLEEP WITH the intention to sleep in and sloth through a rest day, but by 5 o'clock, I'm wide awake and ready to move.

Along the easy trail, I flip up my poles like a swing dance partner to clear the spider webs before digging their rubber feet back into the earth. Dew washes my bare arms. In the saturated earth, a dog's footprints are as deep as mine. Perhaps I shouldn't have grumbled about those sharp rocks two days ago.

By 8 o'clock, my queasy bowels demand attention. I machete deep into the bush, dig a hole, unzip and squat. A twig snaps behind me and a head turn reveals the cause—a Kangal. A second Kangal postures ten feet away.

What does a Kangal think if you shit in his yard? I stare at the ground while covering the hole and creep backwards through the scrubs. I peek under my armpit as I turn forward—he's still watching, but no longer following.

"It's all good buddy, on my way," I say to the frontrunner.

I hopscotch elevated rocks, twisting and erasing four white side-by-side scratch marks etched on each one. The Kangal's cackle silences. The path levels and carves through open, low scrub a 100 feet up from the water, and I float into perceptual monotony. On a desktop globe, this sea-to-sky segment is tinier than a pencil point, making me one-hundredth-of-one-thousandth of a dust particle. Goat bells and tufts of white wool quivering on branches eventually pull me back into my footprints.

Hey look!

"Merhaba!" I call down.

The teenager spins his head right, then left and finally behind him. A fishing pole three times his height counterbalances.

"Hello, swimming?" he yells and waves.

"Hayir," I say as I shake my head. "Likya."

"Likya," he says and points to the path ahead.

"Ekmek?" I'll need food and hope for a market in this next little village.

He nods and returns to casting.

By 10 o'clock, I reach a clearing at sea level and seize the shade of a lone tree. The limbs reach over the water, only possible because of stone embracing the roots. The breeze evaporates sweat from my body and t-shirt as I rest on the natural bench. I use my Swiss Army Knife to cut bread twice the size of a standard sandwich. A triple layer of white cheese and slices from one tomato complete brunch.

Swim? No. But why am I not stopping to even wade?

After 20 minutes, Likya's blatant guidance allows me to dissolve into the wide-angle view and into my music—Rolling Stones, Third Eye Blind, David Gray and Sinéad O'Connor's track 3 from her *How About I Be Me (and You Be You)* album. I don't know most lyrics or titles of any song. Track 3. Side B, fourth song. But songs have impact, one or two lines—an answer to a question, the spark to a future epiphany.

Sinéad starts slow. I leave the trail and climb onto a stone platform the size of a mini trampoline. I sway. A minute in, her guitar intensifies and I join as backup dancer and singer. "One day he'll say, that's my girl. The happiest words in the world." Another minute later, I throw my poles aside and take centre stage. "One day he'll say, that's my girl. The happiest words in the world." After it's over, Sinéad and I give an encore of the same song, twice.

In Boğazcik, boys play soccer across bumpy grass. Two donkeys chase each other along the unpaved main street. A dozen children play on colourful swings, slide and teeter-totter, the first playground I've seen in a village.

"Hello, hello, what is your name?" asks one girl.

"Michelle. What is your name?"

"I am Ela."

"Is there a market, Ela? Bread? Water?"

She points down the road. Did I miss it?

"Hoş geldiniz," a woman says.

"Hoş bulduk," I answer to her welcome. "Yemek?"

"Evet. Çay?" she asks.

"Evet, lütfen."

With an invitation of food and tea, I follow her through a residential gate to a nylon pop-up tent. At a table set in the grass, she serves me tea and mumbles something I don't understand. More women come, all wearing the floral pants, light sweater vests with no sleeves and head scarves. I tuck up unruly hair into my baseball cap. After a round of smiles and merhabas, the women drink tea and chat amongst themselves. My host motions for me to remove my boots and follow her inside. She picks up my backpack one-handed like a lunch box and rests it in the shade against her house. I follow her in, up the staircase and to an outdoor area that overlooks the street. The breeze creates welcome goosebumps. I peek over the low wall but can't see my backpack. Women walk down the street, in singles, in pairs, in small groups. Wait, is that my host? She slams the gate and joins the procession. Is she getting food? Where's everybody going? I feel silly worrying about my pack. After all, she's left me her entire house.

I settle into my viewing deck, with an eye on the village's main square.

1:36pm. Next door in an overgrown yard, an elderly man sitting in a chair slumps forward, only the walking stick in his hand keeps him upright. His head snaps up. Okay, he was just sleeping.

1:38pm. The same spoken word reverberates from a loud speaker in the distance—increasing in volume each time.

1:39pm. On a cement bench, a teenaged girl fixates on her cell phone.

1:41pm. Young men dangle legs off an elevated wooden platform built around a tree and talk to young men sitting on the hoods of cars below.

1:43pm. Stone houses with faded red tile roofs shrink next to new cement houses with outside stairways leading to flat roofs and white plastic chairs.

1:44pm. Faded orange tiles meet pale green and lilac painted walls in my dining room.

1:45pm. My tea is gone.

1:46pm. I sit.

1:49pm. I sit.

1:51pm. I sit.

1:55pm. She's back!

She fills my tea glass, whispers something in Turkish and scurries down the stairs. Chop. Clang. Clink. Men enter the yard, sit at the table in the grass and sip tea. The outdoor speakers blast Turkish music. A young man wearing a red t-shirt and jeans walks up to a middle-aged man in dress pants and shirt, takes his hand and kisses it. Their arms intertwine as they walk through the gate.

"Hello, how are you?" asks the young man.

"Good, thank you, what is the celebration?"

"My friend is getting married."

"A-ha, a wedding."

My host squeezes a massive round tin tray up the tiny stairwell. She moves my tea to make room as she transfers dishes to my table: rice pilaf, fava beans in a tomato sauce, fried eggs in their own two-handled skillet, tomato and green salad, cucumber slices in yogurt and mint, plus a yufka bread larger than a laptop.

"Oh my god, so g-oood." I say.

"Super?" she asks.

"Super duper suuu-per."

Some days, I'm full after a handful of peanuts. Today is not one of them. Today, I eat everything and wipe the plates clean with yufka. After I pay, I suck in my belly enough to fold over to lace up my boots. As I lift on my pack, she asks, "kilograms?" I draw a one and a six on my hand. I'm certain she could lift its numeric opposite. She stops me at the gate to stuff my laminated map deeper into my cargo pocket, snapping it closed while nodding her head.

Back on the trail, my sluggish body hunts for a campsite and finds it within 20 minutes—a flat, grassy area with trees for shade, goats baa-aa-ing plus faint Turkish music from Boğazcik. Wild camping equals freedom. I know this now. Walk until you don't want to walk. But I still struggle with trusting, trusting the right spot will come.

I roll out my sleeping pad and lay in the shade, watching the clouds shift around the sky. Swallows—all tiny birds are swallows—fly into the scene and exit stage left. My journal fills up all afternoon and early evening. No dinner. By 7 o'clock, voices murmur through the trees. Is that German? Hikers can see my camp from the trail, and I love to chat (although it rarely happens). But not tonight. Tonight, I only want to listen to the sky.

DAY 11

Boğazcik to Uçağiz

APPRECIATION WAKES ME. MY equipment and my supplies, my bare essentials, encircle me. The hiking poles wait in the vestibule but everything else camps inside. My backpack curls at my feet. Along the strip of floor beside my sleeping pad, rests my journal, phone/alarm, toilet paper and headlamp. My boots stand single file inside all night—so no need to check for scorpions or spiders—and socks smother the tongues. My baseball cap, sunglasses, bandana, bra, underwear, shirt, MP3 player and daily laminate map hang out in the mesh pocket. My rain jacket and pants mingle behind the kitchen pocket of my pack. Clean village clothes huddle inside my tent's stuff sack and a pink floral scarf wraps around it, creating a camp pillow and giving comfort to my cheeks overnight.

We're moving beyond the awkward introduction stage, Likya and me, and I'm meeting the family.

"Aww, are you sick, Likya?" I ask a fuzzy splotch of red and white paint on a flat rock.

"Hi Grandma Likya." I wave to a neat and tidy but faded waymark, "Oh the hikers you've probably seen, eh?"

Likya babies play on the trail too—all perky and bright. And when a pile of rocks worships a waymark? I meet Famous Second Cousin Likya.

The Likya bugs categorize into new species: the Professional Race Bug that zooms by within a centimetre of my ear. The 911 Bug and its sirens that pull me over, every time. And the Bug-Me Bug—*hey watcha doing? Where ya going? What's in your pack? What does it weigh? Where did you start from today? Got any food? Huh? Do you? Huh?*

The scream of an old goat silences Bug-Me Bug. A kid wails in the distance. Mama Goat and Papa Goat hold vigil on the trail and stare at me.

Kid: Baa-aa-aa-aaaaaa.

Mama: Ba

Kid: Baa-aa-aa-aaaaaa.

Papa: Ba.

Mama waits. Papa waits. I wait. The kid pops onto the trail and together, the family bounces away.

I duck my head and turn sideways through an opening of an ancient stone cottage. A fireplace, like the farmhouse pansiyon, creates the focal point on the left wall. To the right, there's a doorway to another room and a second exit. Swallows fly corner to corner and room to room just inches below the low ceiling. Their brown nest suspends from a centre beam, two feet above my head. The whole nest quivers, and as I get close, I squint and blink to make sense of it.

"Oh shit!"

I pivot and squeeze sideways through the doorway as hundreds of bats flutter by my cheeks. Momentum thrusts me forward into the sunshine while the bats snap left, back into the second doorway. *Oh shit is right, what was THAT thing?* the bats screech back.

After chatting with a German couple hiking for two days—I've yet to meet any thru-hikers—I pinball around human-height jagged rocks and explore sarcophagi, some intact, some with lids overturned exposing the empty grave chambers. The downhill sloping path reveals an inlet and the remnants of the ancient village of Aperlae submerged in turquoise water. Swim amongst crumbling, drowning buildings? (Shutter)

Once at sea level, I cut through a compound—a main house, rooms, campsites, restaurant and couches with folded blankets waiting their evening snuggles. Yellow plastic dump trucks and kiddie cars idle in the yard. A woman coos to a baby inside a small building.

"Camping?" a man asks.

"No, just walking through."

"Drink? Juice?"

"Yes, please, orange?" I give him four lira for the can—overpriced for a city market but thirsty rustic hikers have their own economy. And besides, others pay thousands for their version of equivalent extravagance.

As I walk onwards in the open sunshine, two dozen black goats stampede across the straw-coloured field. Two Kangals, twice a goat's size, trot behind, mouths open, tongues dangling. Thank you Kangals, for keeping the goats safe. Thank you Kangals, for your dedication in this heat. Thank you Kangals, for ignoring me and focusing on your flock.

A quiet café built over the water, indulges me in yet another luxury—a cherry juice this time. The Turkish woman mimes to cut through the fence to find the trail. I cut through the fence. I find the trail. I lose the trail. GPS shows east, yet my book notes say northwest up a hill, then northeast. But GPS rarely talks, so I'm going to listen and move forward along the water, away from the hill. It doesn't feel right though. I turn around and discover two waymarks which seem to backtrack even more, but now amongst boulders, not the open plain.

Back along the water. Back to the hill. Is she laughing at me?

"This is a freaking vortex."

Finally, I bushwhack up the middle, over the hill and turn northeast. I want the ease, the sure-thing, of GPS. But I do love the puzzle of my maps and trail notes. And what about Likya waymarks and the locals? Does it have to be either/or? Can it be all/and? But is that triple the work, second-guessing and re-checking others? I stumble out of the vortex, stuff GPS in a pocket, for now, and reunite with Likya.

Is that Uçağiz in the distance?

Only ten feet from the water, the single-track parallels the edge. The turquoise water tickles the front of the rocks as I weave around the backsides. The round bay floats all sizes of sailboats and Turkish gulets, like a party tray of mixed drinks. Who ordered the 32-foot sloop? The catamaran? Aaand, the micro-cruiser?

The town looks close, yet I never get closer. My soles create a wince with each step. Calves and thighs? Nothing. Back? Shoulders? Nope. Only my soles. When my footsteps stop, my feet are still active—blood flows, lactic acid oxidates, nerves tingle. I invite help once in Uçağiz with a new mantra: *the perfect place, at the perfect price, at the perfect time.*

Uçağiz is six city blocks, no, not even, three city blocks, along a marina of fishing boats, sailboats and gulets. At the market, I buy an orange juice and sit on a stone wall in the shade. At the last sip, a man approaches.

"Hi, how are you, do you need a room?" he asks.

"Maybe, how much for a single room?"

"Fifty lira."

"Hmm, how about 40 lira?"

"Forty lira for a room only or 50 lira with breakfast."

"Perfect."

"Come, I'll show you."

We backtrack along the waterfront to the Baba Veli Pansiyon. We cut through a restaurant, climb up an outside stairwell, and make our way through a wooden doorway to the interior stairwell.

"One is a double, the other a single."

The double room's big balcony faces the back mountains and the single room's tiny side balcony faces the front street and the sea.

"The single is perfect."

"I'll show you the terrace."

Of course there's a rooftop terrace in my perfect place at the perfect price at the perfect time.

I follow him up more stairs and out onto the roof which overlooks the entire waterfront and back mountains.

"Oh wow."

"Cigarette?"

"Evet, thank you, seems I only smoke in Turkey."

"I'm Mehmet," he says as he holds his lighter to my cigarette first.

"I'm Michelle."

Mehmet's tall with dark hair, dark eyes and an open smile. A good-looking man. He works in tourism—Cappadocia in winter, Uçağiz in summer.

"Somebody gives money for their holiday, I take money, then I have a holiday," he says, smiling.

"Nice life, Mehmet. You work just hard enough to enjoy your free time."

"You have a husband?"

"Yes."

"Where is he?"

"In Canada."

"Why didn't he come too?"

"Um, he's, uh, working."

"But you love him?"

"What?"

"You love him?"

I didn't practice that far into the lie. I shrug.

"Ahh." He smiles.

He puts his hand on my arm. "You like wine?"

"Yes."

"Okay, maybe after work, I bring wine and we can have a glass on the terrace, Mehmet and Michelle."

"Okay, um, we'll see, I go to bed early."

I plug in my electronics and check email. I said I wouldn't, but it doesn't feel like work. I'm surprised it doesn't feel like work. And that I don't want to work. I work long and hard, but also too much, like my dad. I love working on my business, but it too easily shifts into people-pleasing and a need to be productive, both prerequisites, it seems, of self-worth. But the last 11 days, I haven't felt that necessity to justify my worth, well, at least not to nature. I don't feel the need to justify my worth to the trees in order to accept their shade. I don't feel the need to justify my worth to the cisterns in order to accept their water. But I still find it awkward to accept the unsolicited generosity of the Turkish people.

At the market, I buy peppers, tomatoes, oranges, bananas, a roll of crackers, a bag of potato chips and two bottles of cold Efes beer. On the terrace, I sip beer and swap stories with a German couple who are walking parts of the Likya. When the wind picks up, I return to my own balcony to finish the cheese and crackers and beer as I write in my journal, and practice Turkish on the potato chip bag.

"Michelle?" Mehmet calls up from a lower floor. He works until nine. He'll bring wine. So we can text, we add each other as contacts on WhatsApp. I like Uçağiz. I like my room. I love my balcony and terrace. And besides, my feet still tingle. I decide to take tomorrow off.

My eyelids get heavy and I check my watch again: 9:20pm. Ten more minutes and I'm turning off the lights. At 9:54pm, my phone beeps.

How are you? texts Mehmet.
Hey, gone to bed, wine another time.
Tomorrow, I'm very busy.
Okay, next time I'm in Turkey then.
Please. Now's a very good time, okay?
No, sorry, sleeping.
Please Please Please.
Nooo. Really. Sleeping.
Please, please. Now? Too early for bed.

I hold my phone in my hands and stare at the screen. Did I want to share a bottle with a good-looking Turkish man earlier tonight? Oh hell yeah. I even shaved my legs. But now? Well, he did offer me the deal on the room. He did give me a cigarette. And he's a very busy man. If I say yes, is it because I feel obligated? Is this how the slide from self starts? What do I want right now? I snuggle further under the white cotton sheets and double-thick cotton bedspread. I tilt my head into the feathery pillow, allowing my right ear to amplify the vibrations of the sea through the open balcony door.

Late for me, goodnight Mehmet. ☺

DAY 12

Uçağiz

ALTHOUGH AWAKE BEFORE SIX, I drift in and out of sleep for four hours. *You're in Turkey, get out of bed.* But I resist. I move to one of two plastic chairs on the balcony and tuck my feet into the wrought iron railing. An empty gulet growls as it reverses in the marina, exchanging positions with the low riding *Haci Baba*, its passengers shoulder-to-shoulder along port and starboard benches. Beneath the balcony, leaves brawl under the lemon tree. Chickens scritch. The lone rooster postures on a wooden ramp, flipping his head back to crow. Sea gulls call out—ke-ow-ha-ha-haa. In the restaurant below, sunburned men in striped polo shirts chatter in English with women in sun hats. Plates and cutlery clink. Turkish hums in the background. Beyond, every boat waves Turkey's flag. I travel light and on a tiny budget, so I don't buy trinkets or souvenirs, except flag pins. In an hour or so, I'll search for one when I walk in to town. Or not.

I twist off a chunk of banana for me and lob a second chunk over the railing. Wait, do chickens eat bananas? The juice from my orange, flows off the table and erodes the grout lines. My feet drench in the juice of two more. I reflect. I write. My journal is near full. I'll buy one in the market, but I will resist the urge to buy two. I don't want the extra weight, so I will trust that the opportunity will come if I need a third. It feels strange, that trust. But I stay in the strangeness.

Without undoing the front button, I slip on my black capri pants. Three and a half feet of my white parachute cord creates a new belt. Nautical. I could live on a sailboat. But there's that knot thing. And navigating, conning and plotting. Oh, and tacking and jibbing. An ex-boyfriend tried to teach me on a sailing dingy but lessons ended after I flipped it (and us) overboard. I signed-up for sailing courses, but the instructors raised their voices in exasperation at my endless questions. My mom sailed her 26-foot sailboat solo, but sometimes I'd join her as an enthusiastic entry-level deckhand. I miss those shared moments of islands and oceans.

Now on the waterfront, I write and sip beer at Ibrahim's Café. A kitten purrs around my ankles, another two stretch out on the stone wall and another three chase servers who shoo them from tables. My kitten knows my beer-only table offers affection only and abandons me as food arrives at the next table. A ragged floppy-eared dog doesn't even get the chance. A server claps his hands the moment one paw touches the patio. People come ashore in the front or arrive from buses in the back. Mehmet hustles in English, German and French (all learned from tourists) and gets people laughing during the 20 seconds it takes to walk the width of the café. Some stay, some go. He's polite. Sweet. Good work ethic. In the lulls between crowds, we continue our conversation.

"Where do the boats come from?" I ask.

"Fethiye or Antalya," he says.

"How long does it take?"

"Two hours."

Two hours for them, 11 days for me.

After a couple of beers, I stroll the waterfront pathway and scan the loaded vendor carts. No flag pins but scarves, t-shirts and jewellery. And a bracelet of *nazar boncuğu*—evil eye beads—concentric circles of dark blue, white, light blue and a centre black dot. A 3000 year old artist tradition but now a popular souvenir, these amulets are meant to ward off evil and protect the wearer, offering peace of mind.

"Merhaba, ne kadar?" I ask.

"Ten," she says.

"Hmm."

"Okay, five."

"Well, that was easy," and dig out five coins.

I explore the docks as a white and orange cat follows, jumping stern to bow of fishing boats moored next to yachts named *Lazy Linda* and *Narcissus*. Uçağiz will be stuffed with people in the summer. Today, it's perfect—enough people to watch and chat with but not overcrowded. I hug Mehmet goodbye, buy food, a beer and the new journal. Buying only one journal doesn't feel strange anymore.

DAY 13

Uçağiz to Andriake

BLANKETS SNUGGLE VENDOR carts. Waterfront cafés sleep, yet are open and vulnerable. The docks rise and fall with each drowsy breath. Should I have stayed? I think I have extra days, where will I use them? I can't calculate or make decisions that far in the future. Can't or don't want to?

I pull at my shoulder straps. Loosen. Tighten. Loosen. I yank my waist belt and fidget with the chest cross strap. My right knee clicks as I loop around a field searching for the way out. Goat paths through scrubs. More fields. Then, the sea.

The bay's boathouse area is a misnomer, only a superstition-inducing cement platform remains. A goat bell on a sailboat echoes, signalling breakfast for the two couples on the deck. I find my own seat on the disintegrating stone wall.

Scrape. Scrape. Scrape.

"Tortoise!"

I offer a piece of apple, but his legs and head retract inwards.

"Not hungry, tortoise? I could nap too, a day off with beer and I'm all out of whack."

The water charms my eyes as my soles bounce off the wall. Ka-thunk, ka-thunk, ka-thunk. Seagulls defy the wind; leaves obey.

The next section is flat, solid dirt which drops me onto an open field.

"Oh, shiii-t."

The four-beat thunder of paws hits me first, a hefty body in pursuit. Warning barks are absent. I spin, scan and grab the only two rocks within reach.

Two hundred feet.

"Please stop. Stopstopstop."

A hundred and twenty feet.

I clench each cannonball.

Eighty feet.

"Hey! Heyy-a-heyyy!"

Forty feet.

The first rock lobs and thuds nine feet away.

Twenty feet.

I drop the other rock, turn sideways and fake-yawn with exaggerated lip licks, the canine calming signals are worth a try. He slows to a trot, and barks as he circles behind me. I shuffle in inches, head down. Fake-yawning.

"Kangal Kangal, puppy puppy." It calms me, but does it mock him? He marches me straight out of the field.

"Sorry sir, going, wouldn't have actually hit you."

After another 50 shuffles, he's beyond peripheral vision. At last peek, he's lying across the path at the edge of the field.

Stand down. Crisis averted.

I'm thirsty, but my shaking hands can't open or manoeuvre the bendy water tube yet.

An hour on, I weave along a wall of stacked rocks, but slow movement within it lures me in. I focus on a rectangular opening, a little bigger than my MP3 player. The movement quickens. The snake's cream and black colouration pattern is blurry, like newspaper in a fast-forward microfilm reader.

"Whooo-weee," I say to match the first two seconds.

"Whooa," I whisper in baritone, as the slither speeds up for the next three, four, five seconds.

Now hypnotized like a reverse snake charm, I watch in silence as the slithering intensifies within the hollow rock wall, and after six, seven, eight more seconds, I tip toe backwards, comprehending the snake's full length.

I haven't seen or heard anyone in four hours when a *hello* from behind vaults me off the trail as a runner in blue flashes by.

"Oh wow, cool, enjoy your run!"

I should've said, Hey, wait, running the Likya? You're my kind of guy! I'd love my guy to ask me: *Hey Michelle, want to road trip to Nicaragua?* Yes! *Hey Michelle, want to run the Camino de Santiago del Norte?* Definitely! *Hey Michelle, want to cycle-camp the United States coastlines?* Wait, with my dog? *Wouldn't go any other way.* Yes, absolutely!

At the junction, a low rickety bridge made of tree limbs, two-by-fours and blue painted boards drops me onto a long curve of white sand, bordered by sand dunes and a gentle bay. Swim? No. Camp? Too exposed. Food? I walk into town, although it's more like a wharf area where tour busses park beside gulets and the party boats that had drilled through my silence the last hour.

One café, one tiny market. I buy a can of cherry juice and one-and-a-half litres of water, which fills up my bladder pack. I buy another bottle of water and the market guy points to the garbage can. Do they recycle?

"Ekmek?" I ask.

"Hayir."

No bread. Only water, potato chips, peanuts (I still have some) and tubs of cheese. Unsure of my next step, I sit in the shade and sip water.

"Ekmek," says the market owner and points to a white panel van that jumps the curb and parks on the sidewalk. A silver-haired man fills the outdoor wood and glass cabinet with a dozen loaves of warm bread.

"One lira" he says.

In the middle of the river overpass stands a chubby Kangal puppy about four months old. Ears back, tail tucked, body low, but when I kneel down and turn sideways, he comes to me with a bum wiggle. My fingertips spider-walk down his back, flicking off one tick but others hang on tight.

"You want to hike with me, little Kangal?"

He rests his squishy chin on my one bent knee and looks up. He has a collar, which means a home. But do I pick off his ticks and give him a bath and food anyways? Would he then follow me? I don't want him to. Or do I? It's been 15 months since Monty died. Am I ready for another dog?

Together, we walk down the steps, and he flop-trots into the sand. He stops, spins to chase his tail, then flop-gallops towards the water.

"Okay, bye little Kangal."

I backtrack along the beach, cross the low rickety bridge, turn right at the trail junction and climb. My feet are tender on the sharp rocks, and I search for the first flat spot. I step off the trail a few times to survey potential sites barely the size of my tent, but with no room to walk around without stepping on rocks, I move on. Sweat rolls into my eyes. After 40 minutes, I discover it—a flat space under a tree that will accommodate my tent and walk-about space, and it has a bonus sea view.

Camp priorities begin with #1—switch from boots to flip flops. Priority #2—switch from sweaty clothes to dry, airy camp clothes. Priority #3—roll out sleeping pad and rest, elevate feet if possible.

The breeze cools me but not enough to stop sweating. Changing into my swimsuit top helps. Once I lie down on the sleeping pad, the breeze disappears. I sit up for breeze—30 seconds—then lie down to elevate my feet—30 seconds. Up for breeze, down for feet. After a dozen sequences, I'm cool enough to stay horizontal for the next half-hour and relax to nature's noise.

It's 3 o'clock, and bedtime will be at about 9 o'clock, or whenever it gets dark. So that's six hours of nothing to do, but somehow the time passes by. Set up camp. Lounge. Unpack, repack. Sit. Set up battery pack for GPS/phone. Write. Make dinner. Stretch. Explore. Review maps and routes. Write. Stare at the sky.

While writing, a team of yellow and black grasshoppers stalks me. One creeps towards me. I throw a pebble nearby, and it jumps back three feet. Another team member creeps forward, and I strike back with a pebble. It retreats with a jump just as another team member takes over. C'mon, what do I have that you want?

While reviewing maps and routes, I peek ahead to the final two-day mountain pass. Should I do it? Not sure. If I wait, maybe the decision will make itself. There's no point in worrying, but it's too late. I'll need tunes now to loosen the unease before sleep comes.

Breathing. I pause my dream. Was that me breathing? No. It's behind my head. A slow inhale. A slow exhale. My eyelids snap open in bursts of threes, and my fingers stretch for my hiking pole. Stay in or burst out? Staying in relies on three millimetres of nylon for protection. Bursting out involves a zipper first, giving it a two-second head start. A head start to run away? Or attack? I sit up and fumble for the zipper.

Snort. Snort.

Snort-snort-snort.

Snort? Wild boar!

I back flop onto my sleeping bag, and my adrenaline plummets. I giggle and snort alongside the boar while fumbling for my flashlight. Wait, illuminate a wire-haired feral swine with fangs? I drop my flashlight, cuddle my makeshift pillow and fall asleep to the cheery snorts of chubby pink piglets with twisted tails.

DAY 14

Andriake to Belören

BY 8AM, I LOSE THE TRAIL. I backtrack to the last waymark and scan for rock piles, perimeter boulders and trees in the middle of the field for hints of red and white paint. I shift forward to change my perspective. Nothing. First step, scan. Second step, review the narrative and maps. Third, GPS. I've been engaging GPS in conversation all morning. It's been chatty, but it's saying a whole lot of nothing. Why does that piss me off? Why can't I turn it off if it's not helping? Why do I keep demanding answers from a source that's not giving? If I'm focused on it, am I missing easy answers from other sources? I've asked for help from other sources, sometimes frantically. But even then, I don't want to be told everything. I don't want the full answer. Just a little guidance. Hints.

Okay, GPS says the trail is north. As I bushwhack, branches tease my hair from a ponytail into a witch-do. Boulders test arm and leg strength as I yank myself up and over, while branches reach lower to jab-jab-jab and finally slam me with a right hook.

"Come on, seriously!"

I look back often, but that last waymark finally vanishes. Trees exhale, I gasp. Twenty more minutes pass by. Wait—I press my ear into vibrations. Cars? I hike one last hill and drop onto a farmer's field—a greenhouse to the left, a road to the right. Beyond the road, there's a yellow Likya sign with arrows for Sura, along the road, or for Myra, back into the mountains. I choose Myra and scramble up a narrow gorge and navigate around naked boulders, no waymarks. This doesn't feel right. Where's the trail? No GPS, no waymarks, and a bad feeling. I backtrack to the empty road and, ah perfect, I'll ask these two village women.

"Merhaba," I say. Nothing.

Did they hear me? As they walk closer, I wave.

"Merhaba," I say again. No smiles.

Silent, they both step to their right to block my way. They glare, and one rubs her thumb over her middle and index finger.

"Money? You want money? No." My face reflexes into disbelief as I step around them.

Wait, did I misunderstand? I turn around and their eyes fixate on my hand as I pull a five lira note from a cargo pocket.

"You wanted money?"

One woman reaches for it.

"*Hayir!* No!" I yell and snatch it away. An intimidating, but rare occurrence, and a reminder of my vulnerability.

The side road dead-ends at the main four-lane highway. Left, Kaş; right, Demre and Antalya. The main highway has a narrow shoulder but not many cars or trucks. Do I walk north towards Kaş and hope for a Likya sign near the highway? Or catch a dolmuş to Demre, and walk north to Myra to rejoin the trail? I dump my pack, sit on a concrete block, and wait for the decision.

A man appears in the doorway of a building.

"Dolmuş to Demre?" I ask while crossing the street to him.

"Evet."

"Dolmuş?" I point to the side of the road, and stick out my arm as if flagging it down.

"Evet" and holds up five fingers.

Five minutes? Five kilometres? Five lira?

"Ne Kadar?"

"Icki," and holds up two fingers.

"Dolmuş?" and point at 9:45 then 9:50 then 9:55 on my watch.

"Evet."

Okay, two lira, every five minutes, and I just flag it down. I think.

"Teşekkür ederim," I say and I return to the concrete post. Maybe I'll just walk to Demre? On my not-to-scale map, Demre looks five kilometres away.

A few minutes later, the same man drives by in a flatbed truck with foot-high stake sides. A man and a woman squeeze beside him in the front and a third man squats in the open back.

"Demre," says the driver and points to the back.

"Evet! Teşekkür ederim!" Despite investigating hundreds of motor vehicle accidents, I'll never pass up an invitation to ride in the open back of a truck.

I fling my poles over and hoist up my pack as the man in the back helps. I step on the rear tire, swing my legs over and stumble into place as the truck merges onto the highway. My left hand rests on the low sides, but after losing games of hand-slap with the cliff's guard rail, tucks inside. *Look beyond, not over and down.* The sea's high definition turquoise, the wind's hum and the truck's loose suspension lull me into meditation. Fifteen minutes later, it's over.

"Teşekkür ederim," I say as I dig for money but the driver shakes his head and waves.

Jackhammers drill concrete. Hammers pound nails. Men in hard-hats yell to other men in hard-hats. Men in suits on cell phones weave around women pushing strollers. Vendors in a pedestrian mall hawk pide, snacks and coffee. Trinkets hang in windows, t-shirts flap in doorways and tourist books spin on wire racks. At a market, the aisles mutate into a midway, the products into carnies—try eight kinds of soap! Pasta! Chocolate bars! Electrical cords! Bare fluorescent tubes flicker and buzz as I fixate on the back cooler, grab the closest juice, drop lira on the counter and flee to a lone tree sapling growing out of concrete.

Eventually, I toss yesterday's map, old bread and a wad of toilet paper into a garbage bin and submit to urbanization.

A bank machine faces the sidewalk, and I join the line. I still have cash I had exchanged at home but I never trust that bank cards will work across the world, so I might as well try this one now. Through the English prompts, I request 700 lira, enough for two weeks. It works! I walk inside, stand and stare. How does this work? What do I do? I feel silly.

"Merhaba. *Kü-çük? Yir-mi?* Lütfen?" I ask a woman in a business suit and nametag. Small? Twenty? Please?

"Evet," she says and pulls a number from the ticket machine by the front door. How'd I miss that?

"Merhaba, küçük, yirmi, lütfen?" I ask the teller, who exchanges my hundreds for twenties.

Tomato greenhouses surround me. Heat from the open windows blasts sweat from my arms like a car wash dryer. Likya hides, but a tour bus passes. So I'm probably walking towards Myra. After the greenhouses, I pass homes again, with orange trees higher than roofs. What's the penalty for fruit theft?

With so many houses, a market will soon appear. I buy a hunk of white cheese, two packages of peanuts, a large water, a loaf of fresh bread, a canned juice and a roll of chocolate chip cookies.

"*Meyve? Sebze?*" The clerk shakes his head (no fruits or vegetables) and points back to Demre.

Next door at the second market, I buy another juice and ask, "*Domates?*"

He shakes his head. My smiley face crashes. But wait. His index finger wiggles as he disappears down a narrow aisle. What's he got? He returns with a plastic bag of tomatoes. He glances around the empty market as he selects 20 bite-size tomatoes plus two green peppers. I slide him three coins, bury my loot, whisper thank you and slip out the door.

The asphalt reduces to construction gravel, and when I squeeze to the side of the road to make room for a dump truck, my boots sink into greyness. Well, this would make drowning imminent. I hunch over my boots and scrape wet cement out of each crevice with a stone blade. With both boots excavated, I continue until I see a man in jeans and t-shirt leaning on a barricade, holding a sign—*DUR*. Stop. Police line? Traffic diversion?

"Okay?" I ask.

"Evet."

I duck under the barricade, round a corner and continue north until a backhoe digging a trench blocks the street. A man standing guard presses himself against the wall, and I squeeze between him and the grunting backhoe.

I cross a bridge over the river, and there are still no Likya signs—none since early this morning. *Turn left and walk towards the mosque until the pavement ends,* says the book. Am I on the road where the pavement ends? This road parallels the river—now, barely a stream—with houses in front of greenhouses on the right and goat shacks on the left. Chickens and roosters are in the middle.

A grandma sweeping a driveway waves me over.

"Hello, merhaba." I say as I approach.

She waits for me with one muscular arm resting on a hip, her posture straighter than the homemade broom. Her silver hair sticks out from under the head scarf, and her soft eyes and smile lure me in. I follow her to a concrete shed where she stops at the doorway shorter than her and points inside.

Does she have tea?

My eyes adjust to the dark—a single window, dirt floor, fireplace, four women. And a heap of flat bread.

The first woman, sitting on the floor, scoops dough from a plastic basin, kneads it and passes it to the next woman, also sitting on the floor, who pounds it flat on a wooden table. She flops it onto the next table, and the third woman rolls it thin with an *oklava*—a Turkish rolling rod. The fourth woman sends the yufka into the open fire, and when it's done, flings it onto the heap.

Grandma picks up a red pepper and declares something in rapid Turkish. How does she know I'm classically conditioned to stop, drop and eat at roasted red peppers and flat bread?

A younger woman—grandma's daughter—turns a white plastic crate over. Grandma also sits on a crate and taps my knee as we huddle in the doorway. Two grandsons hide behind their mom's floral pants as she sets a tray of glasses on the ground and pours a round of colas. Grandma builds a pyramid of salt then passes the tray into the cement room. It returns with charred peppers and a yufka.

"Oo, ahh, oo, ahh." I say, as I juggle a pepper. The grandsons giggle into their hands. Grandma grabs the peppers and peels the burned skin with steady hands. She unfolds the yufka, presses the two peppers flat, adds salt, wraps it up and burrows it into my hands.

"Oh my, oh my, yu-uuum."

The boys giggle louder, so I go louder.

"Yum yum yuuu-ummm yum yum yum."

The boys pull their shirts over their faces. Grandma smiles too. I turn on my phone to translate *best lunch ever*, but Grandma bounces her palm off her chest and poses, knuckles digging into her hips. I take her photo, of course, and she approves of it with a nod and a double wink.

With permission, I take a photo of the four women making yufka, and my phone crowd surfs into the room. Grandma tries to dust it off, but I shake my head and sniff the pink case covered in flour and smoke.

I offer money for my lunch, but all refuse. Grandma and I hold hands before she slips them free to wrap me in a hug.

"Teşekkür ederim, güle güle," I say to the four women inside who haven't stopped working.

"Good. Bye," they say, smiling and waving.

The dirt road cuts through cement houses and greenhouses. One man heel-toes across a roof, balancing on the metal seams around the square glass panels. I acknowledge his courage with a smile. He smiles and points to his head. Is that *I'm crazy* or *don't worry, I'm using my head?*

Soon, a yellow sign for Belören directs me between a greenhouse and a home.

A woman sweeping asks, "Likya? Evet," and points to the gap in the buildings.

It feels like I'm trespassing in full view, but it works and soon I'm climbing stone switchbacks until I reach the cistern that the book mentions. Gravity pulls me into a right turn, but soon it feels wrong. Too long with no waymark. At the first house, two little terriers charge, circle and bark. Although small, I stand still until someone comes out of the house to shoo them away.

"Likya? Belören?"

"Belören," he says and points up the hill.

I want to thank him for collecting his dogs. I want to thank him for the directions. But without words or a smile, I turn around and shuffle back up the steep asphalt for the next half-hour. At the mark of my initial right turn, I stay on the road. Around the bend, there's a cement cistern and a yellow sign directly above it—*Belören 4 kms*. This is the cistern to mark the right turn, not the other cistern. I melt into it. Should I camp here? *On a cistern at the side of the road?* Well, I could. Okay, slow it down. First, water.

I remove the wood cover and peer into the dark hole. Is that a lizard? I learned how to use my sister's water filter on the West Coast Trail and bought the same one, one less thing to learn. I loop my parachute cord around the plastic lid of my water bottle and tie eight half knots. Yeah, eight. I know, I know. The bottle drops to the water, floats for a second, then sinks. Okay, no bugs that I can see, but there are floating particles bigger than I want to drink. I screw the filter onto my water pack, feed its plastic tubing into the well water in the water bottle and yank the handle up. The filter pops off and water gushes under my thighs, soaking my pants.

"Fuuu-ck."

I twist it back on and wrestle it with a single-hand choke hold as I crank the handle again. It squirms out of my grip and jumps off the cistern.

"You stupid, shii-it!" I yell as I throw my half-filled water bottle at the fleeing filter.

Filtering water is a simple task, except when proceeded by backtracking in full sun at the end of the second week of a 500-kilometre trail. Backtracking proceeded by excavating boot treads. Excavation proceeded by two extorting village women. Extortion proceeded by a cheeky GPS and trickster waymarks. But, I remember the generosity of the man with the flatbed truck. I remember the fire-roasted peppers on yufka shared with three generations. I remember the merchant who shared his stash of beloved tomatoes. I remember the private campsites with sea views. And I remember that I'm on holidays. For a month. In Turkey.

Go slow. I dunk the bottle again. The filter twists onto the water pack attachment with slow half-turns, and then I release my grip to lift the filter handle with my thumb and index finger only. Up. Down. I add the weight of my hand. Up. Down. I dunk the bottle again.

Thank you parachute cord, thank you filter, thank you water bottle and thank you full cistern of water.

Across the road, I squeeze into the dusty notch of a mountain. The breeze bails, but heat lingers. Every few feet, my handkerchief stretches from my neck to my forehead to wipe the sweat. My boots resist the overtime and sloppily pivot off loose rocks sending them flying, like a pissed-off cubicle worker knocking a stapler off this desk, coffee mug off that one. The scree slopes up the first 30 feet, dark green smearing the mountain above. Wait, is that a terrace? My tracks vanish behind me as I climb the debris to the flattened area.

Eight hundred metres above the sea, shepherds call out. Goats on the right of the gorge yell to goats on the left, like neighbours gossiping across balconies. I squint at the white woolly dots, like ellipses on a green chalkboard. The sun vaults over, through and around Demre's white buildings, finally dropping to the sea before rolling back to Point A.

Goat bells ring close. Closer. A herd of eight grabs at branches as they amble up the sloping terrace. I set down my journal, lean back into my Therma-a-Rest chair and pull up my knees to balance my cell phone. I bow my head but track them with my eyes.

Breathe.
Ding-ding. Ding
Breathe.
Ding. Ding.

The goats keep coming. Ten feet. Six feet. At two feet away, I push down my shoulders. The goats stop. I hold my breath. A hoof taps the sleeping pad. A black goat with bite chunks out of both ears stares down the bridge of his raised nose like a Supreme Court judge.

"Mer-ah-baaaa," I whisper during an exhale.

I grip my camera tighter, less a desire to capture the moment and more the need to occupy my hands that yearn to touch. A kid nibbles my rainfly until the mama startles us both with her BAA-AA-AAAA. The Supreme-Court-Goat adds another hoof to the sleeping pad and stares. I slide one finger onto the screen—gotcha. The kid bucks and twists, the adults meander next, the Supreme-Court-Goat at the rear.

I opted against a Turkish SIM card but will my Canadian SIM card work? Can I get cell phone coverage up here? I test it. The answering machine comes on—it's 8:30 in the morning there.

"Uh, hi Dad, it's Michelle. I'm camping on top of a mountain tonight, so thought I'd see if my phone works, which it does, so thought I'd say hello, so hello, anyways, see you soon."

I pluck my hiking clothes from the bushes, and while standing on my sleeping pad, I shake plant remnants off my pants and watch as tiny black ants sprinkle all over the tomato colour mat.

"Well, that explains how they get in the tent."

A new evening ritual begins.

Writing? Check. Bedroom set-up? Dinner? Underwear-in-a-bag bath and laundry? Check.

I sit on my sleeping pad. Just sit. Sit and gaze as the sea disappears behind clouds. Mist floats below the clouds and approaches like the goats. Twenty feet. Fifteen feet. At ten feet, I fade into the mist for one last pee before I crawl into my tent and zip out the silence.

It's only 800 metres. I don't have a stove for tea. It changed so fast. I suck at building fires. Do I even have matches? I don't think I have matches. I must have matches. Of course I have matches. Wait, do I? When duck down gets wet, it stays wet. *Hypothermic woman found in wet sleeping bag, alone.* I'll look like an asshole if I call search and rescue.

Maybe I won't climb the mountain tomorrow. *That's cheating.* Is that cheating?

I wake at 2:19am, and the wind whips against my rain fly. From my stuff sack pillow, I pull out my last shirt and for the first time, zip my sleeping bag hood over my head. Every hour, I wake up with coiled legs in the corner of my tent as the mountain continues its attempts to slide me off.

DAY 15

Belören to Finike

T HE RISING SUN WARMS MY sleeping bag, heat therapy for tightness that stretches along my soles and over the Achilles tendon.

By 8 o'clock, I dismantle the rock cairn as my feet dangle over the terrace wall. Forwards or backwards? Hurl the pack first? When I lean forward, my pack shoves me off the ledge.

"Whoa, whoa, whoa."

Like an Arctic icebreaker, I slide through the scree until a boulder catches me—*boom*—back on the trail.

"Mer-a-baaa! Hoş geldiniz!" he screams, then pumps my hand as he gives me a cheek-to-cheek kiss. "Italiana?"

"Hoş bulduk, Canada."

"Caaa! Naaa! Daaa!"

Men congest instead of cars as we chat in Belören's only intersection.

"Su?" I ask and point to the cistern.

"Evet," says another man.

I unclip my straps, but Great Big Welcome Man points behind a wire fence. He disappears through a stone house, reappears in the chicken yard and plugs in the pump as the second man uses a hose to fill my hydration pack. Wanting to stock up, I dip my extra water bottle into the overflow bucket.

"No no noooooo!" they both yell, one swats my hand, and Great Big Welcome Man points to a goat. They smile, I blush, we all laugh.

On the steep rocky road out of the village, a Peugeot spins tires in low gear. A woman lugs long grass on her back from below her hips to above her head.

"Likya," she says and points straight up the hill.

Likya leads me until a decision: *Myra 10km* or *Finike 29km*.

Left—a wolf-dog. Right—a village woman. As I pass her, she shakes my hand as her thin lips pull back into a one-incisor smile.

The temperature drops as I flop down towards Alakilise, but sweat still stings my eyes. Flies hitchhike on my face, and to continue non-stop pole swings, I contort my lips to aim my exhales and blast them off.

The Alakilise ruins appear through the pine valley, but it's the mountain above that captivates. *Do not climb alone as mountains are totally isolated and deserted in April and May,* I recall from my guidebook. It's been hours since I saw the village woman, and I'm not even close to the 1700 metre peak. Is that a road up there? I check my map, yes, a road. My heart beats as if I'm already climbing.

Before I left home, my mind was active—*you can't write a book about the trail if you don't hike the whole trail. You scared of a little mountain?* But now? Absent. The inner chatter gets loudest just before you step out of your comfort zone. But once you step out, it quietens. My feet carry me towards the mountain, and stop. I'm not writing about the trail, I'm writing about my experience with the trail. I turn around but peek back as the mist drops, hiding the mountain. Okay yeah, I'm scared, but more mountains will come.

After Belören, the trail back to my previous terrace campsite invites me. Backtrack? Or walk the road to Demre? A four-door FIAT passes and stops. A back door flings open.

"Demre?" I ask.

Four women get out, open the trunk and make room for my pack next to gallon jars of olives and together, we squish back in. Within minutes, I car-dance to the blast of Dance Hits Volume One, and soon we're all getting down while getting down.

"What is your name?" my seatmate yells.

"Michelle, and your name?"

"Semra!"

"Günsel!"

"Damla!"

"Rabia!" yells the driver as she veers right, creating extra room for an oncoming cube van.

Around another curve, Demre reveals itself in the valley below, and Rabia skids to the rocky shoulder. Ride over? They pile out and stand arm-in-arm where a guard-rail would be—photo op—then wave me into the frame too.

Once in Demre, they point out windows, flag over pedestrians, and after two more left-right-lefts, Rabia slides into a parking lot and presents the bus terminal with a double-arm sweep.

In the bathroom, two teenagers fiddle with clothes and practice selfie smiles as I dig out a clean shirt despite recent underwear-in-a-bag showers.

"Finike?" I ask a bus driver.

"*Besh*," he says and I hand over five lira, proud that I know my numbers.

He loads my pack and points to a back row seat between a round Turkish woman and a thin, young man. *Internet ba123456* reads a sign above the driver's seat. Wi-Fi? I clear my business inbox, email my sister and my dad, upload a photo to Facebook and squeeze my phone back into my cargo pocket. We're off on Highway 400, a seaside highway that begs for more motorcycles.

Thirty minutes later, the driver turns into Finike—the noise of cafés, scooters and moms with crying babies in strollers all flood onto the bus as I fight my way off.

Slow it down. Sit. Adjust. Stay tonight? Take a bus tomorrow, up the mountain to the trail? Camp on the outskirts? Walk it out.

The seaside promenade is a dance floor of Turkish couples—women in tight white pants and pink high-heels, men in tan slacks and shirts with no ties. Arm-in-arm couples smile and nod. I smile back and embrace my collapsed hiking poles as I try to ignore the dirt exploding under my boots like Godzilla. After 15 minutes, the beach shops and cafés with Turkish-only menus end and a sign confirms it—*Finike Güle Güle.*

I pass a school and an electric company, each with a *Baykal Pansiyon* sign tied to the chain link fence. Along the seaside, stands a lone red building with plastic tables in the sand and a sign on the roof—*Beach Café.* After ten minutes of industrial buildings, I see another *Baykal Pansiyon with wifi* sign. There it is on the corner, across from an empty lot with idling semi-trucks—the Baykal Pansiyon. If it's less than 30 lira, I'm staying.

Curtains block the ground floor windows so I open the door to investigate and feel comfortable alongside a mom, dad and baby who watch sports on a TV hung above an empty bar.

"Merhaba," I say to the family and the man in the office. "Pansiyon, bir?"

"Twenty-five lira," he says in English. "Do you want to see?"

We step over a white and brown dog asleep in the sunbeam. "He's security."

He shows me a room with a spotless tile bathroom, two double beds, a fridge and a small balcony facing an inner courtyard.

"Laundry?"

He nods. Done.

The beach café is empty except for four servers sitting at a table.

"Evet?" I ask as I point to an outside table.

"Evet, evet," says one man as he jumps up to grab a menu.

The 50 or 60 patio chairs are empty and I relax into a beachfront seat. Tires painted white surround the bases of palm trees while lights in clear globes connect tree to tree.

"Do you speak Turkish?" he asks in English.

"No, sorry."

He opens the Turkish menu and points to the items. "We have kebabs, chicken, beef."

"Hayir et lütfen, sebze?" I ask.

"No meat, okay, vegetables, yes, vegetarian."

He names some vegetables, I think, and I add bread. "Bira?"

He shakes his head.

Fifteen minutes later, he returns with a board with an iron skillet full of grilled vegetables—potatoes, green and red peppers, tomatoes, eggplant. Another wooden board bigger than my dinner plate balances a fire-roasted flat bread, edges stretch to the checked tablecloth.

"Oh my oh my."

He laughs as he adds a goblet of fresh-squeezed orange juice. I scatter course salt on everything, including the bread and dig in.

Beach, food, juice, handsome server, and oh look, a dog.

A hefty, white dog with a black eye patch plays tag with an imaginary playmate before darting out of view. Well-fed, collar on, neutered. The dog sprints back into view, holding his head high to prevent his treasure—a clear plastic bag stuffed with garbage—from smacking the beach recliners as he hurdles.

Look! Look! Look! as he glances sideways. I know that look. I shared it not five minutes before.

"Coffee?"

"Çay lütfen, tea please."

Was it only 14 days ago when ordering tea brought on a stint of travel anxiety? I sip my tea as I end the evening captivated by a random piece of white tissue whirling in a vortex eight feet off the ground.

DAY 16

Finike

WALK. SIT. WRITE. WALK. Garbage cans overflow. Cigarette butts disappear somewhere. Kids play on swings while moms line up at ice cream vendors. White tiled public bathrooms everywhere, and I still choose the western toilet. Families. Parks. Clean.

Men fish in the canal. Reeds ripple at the bottom like the tresses of a face-down water goddess. Scooters lurch up ramps and cross the canal beneath floral arches. Five-story apartment buildings painted pink, peach, yellow and white—Turkish flags drape over at least one balcony per story. Walkways. Flowers. Community.

Walk. Sit. Write. Walk.

A farmer's market squeezes between apartment buildings—red peppers! Almonds! Dried fruit! One kid sells me two handfuls of apricots, another a banana, while still another three oranges, a tomato and cucumber. Fresh, local food. Friendly vendors. How much are rental apartments?

Walk. Sit. Write. Walk.

As I sip an Efes on my balcony, I ponder the past 24 hours. Yesterday, I was assaulted with Finike's noise and today, I want to live here.

DAY 17

Finike to Karaöz

A MAN GRIPPING A FLASHLIGHT slouches in a chair, his head pins a pillow to the wall. As I squeeze by, my pack smacks his shoulder, but he doesn't wake or even move. I tiptoe down the stairs, through the dark lobby and out into the sunshine. Security Dog opens one eye to see who is blowing him kisses before readjusting his lounge position.

"You need a hammock, dog."

Instead of walking on the beach sand, I start on the brick seaside walkway, wider than a road lane. A 100 feet to my right, waves compete for the attention of both the sun and the moon.

Click-clack, click-clack.

It's Sunday. Only one car a minute and a few random people in shaded bus stops. One man hands me an orange as he points down the road.

By 8 o'clock, I plug into my MP3 player's shuffle mode, and first song up is Train's "I'm About to Come Alive." Tears and wails blast out like a Beatles fan circa 1964. What the hell is this?

Don't give up on me, I'm about to come alive

—Train, "I'm About to Come Alive"

Still? I don't want this journey to be about men, I want it to be about my dog. But I know we don't get to choose. Whatever comes up, needs healing.

"Okay, fine, you want to go there? I'll go there. You really wanna go there? Let's fucking go there then."

I pound the down-arrow to Train, a favourite band I've skipped over for four years. I walk while reliving the memories.

He was a police officer too. We worked the same patrol district and later, created undercover and surveillance projects together. On days off, we'd share long nights making love and shadow puppets. After two years, he moved in.

And did you miss me while you were looking for yourself out there?
   —Train, "Drops of Jupiter"

Whenever he heard our song, "Drops of Jupiter"—in a store, on his car's radio—I'd find a recorded snippet on my answering machine. I'd do the same on his pager, even as I travelled alone through Ecuador.

Everybody needs a little time
   —Train, "Respect"

My one-bedroom apartment squeezed in his two young kids every second weekend for the next five years. I loved our Disney movie nights and creating birthday treasure hunts, but I ignored my need for alone time to re-charge energy.

They call her Mississippi

But she don't flow to me
       —Train, "Mississippi"

When I resigned from our shared career to start my own dog training business, I sensed we wouldn't survive the transition. The drift started soon after. In response, I scheduled even later client appointments and more weekend events, while he accepted a 24/7, on-call position. *I have to work* replaced *I love you.*

I don't know if I can wait this long
To be what I used to be
       —Train, "I Wish You Would"

In the final two years, I shifted into desperation. Not consciously, but upon reflection. I stopped saving for international travel and going on weekend road trips to wait at home in case he didn't have to work. After 20 years of a vegan diet, I started eating cheese, chicken and fish in an attempt to deepen our connection over rare shared meals. *Great barbecue salmon, sweetie!* Sex slipped off. *I'm too tired. Yeah, me too.* And I sat on the chair, he sat on the couch, as we drank beer and watched *Cops*, ending my six-year, no-TV peace.

It's all better now, things are gonna work somehow
       —Train, "Something More"

One day, he answered my phone call—*oh, hey there*—the words and flat tone reserved only for his ex-wife. Later, while I waited and munched chicken nuggets by myself in front of his TV, a moment of clarity—*who the fuck am I?*

And I know this could be

That free fall back to me
  —Train, "It's About You"

Without knowing how to communicate my needs, I didn't include him in my return to self. I booked a hotel in Seattle for a solo weekend getaway. I reopened a savings account for travel. When he turned the TV on, I listened to my MP3 player's headphones on the patio. I bought my own vegan groceries. Within six months, I asked him to move out. But I didn't want to end the relationship. I only wanted temporary breathing space. Four months later, I helped him move into his own apartment, but he moved even further and married within a year.

Cry. Breathe.

Keep going.

But I'm over him, so what's with the tears?

This isn't about him, it's about you.

Hurt. Loss. Grief.

And longing for connection.

My thoughts float to my dad. My sister had planned a goodbye dinner. I drove because Dad had been drinking scotch. The drinking wasn't a problem before, but had escalated during the six months after his wife died.

While we stood in the driveway, I had second-thoughts about going inside. It triggered memories of being the person who used to drive my mom around when she was drinking. It took me too many years to learn how to set boundaries with my mom when she drank. But seeing my dad every day, I had become closer to him in the last six months than in the past 40 years, and I didn't want to risk pushing him away.

I intended to explain my concerns for his health, compassion for his grief and how much we loved him. Those thoughts were shared, along with shouts and tears—all mine, ignited by fear and apprehension about the hike. My dad's earlier smile disappeared, and with his head down, he whispered, "Michelle, take me home."

Hold up my wings 'cause you are the sky
　　— Train, "Eggplant"

That night, he stayed in the computer room while I stayed in the spare bedroom, packing and unpacking three times, maybe four. The next morning, we drove to the airport and hugged in silence, without looking at each other.

I believe in love
I believe in love
　　—Train, "Blind"

Cry. Breathe.
Hurt. Loss. Grief.
And longing for connection.
I finally stand still and hold my poles in one hand as I swipe tears with the other. I scramble down the embankment to the empty beach. My pack slumps to the sand, and I lay flat, stretching out my legs, arms too, staring up. As I wiggle, the sand makes room for me, and the volume cranks as I stare up, way up, through the sky.

Take my hand in the meantime
And let's walk into the sunshine
Everybody got something that they want to sing about, laugh about, cry about
It's true
For me it's you

—Train, "For Me it's You"

Cry. Breathe. Sing.

"Take my hand in the meantime, and let's walk into the sunshine, everybody got something that they want to sing about, laugh about, cry about, it's true, for me it's you."

"For me, it's you."

"Na na na na, na na, na na na."

"For me, it's you."

Inhale. Exhale.

As muscles relax further into the sand, I switch back to shuffle mode. First song? "Transformation."

Transformation has begun
We're walking but our feet,
don't touch the floor,
    —David Gray, "Transformation"

I laugh out loud. Really, loud out loud, belly-bouncing loud, out loud. "Well, that's a lot before ten in the morning."

I cross the bridge and back to the waterfront where jagged asphalt edges meet sand and scrub bushes. Row after row, stilted houses stand at ease, shutters closed, porch roofs saluting. Basketball courts, rusted hoops and bleachers sit empty. Where is everybody?

A dead end steers me left between two houses and I slice the reeds along a river. Likya has withheld guidance since Finike, but my book says go east for six hours. So if I always choose right turns and hug the sea, I'll eventually get to Karaöz.

Hundreds of greenhouses, no cars, minimal shade, sporadic water taps. I turn right on a side road to the beach and veer left with the sidewalk through the open gate of a community of duplexes, *Phase Three—not yet complete.* Fancy imported sedans. Manicured lawns. Pink flower infused trees line tiled walkways across the sand to beach huts at the water's edge. Without people to watch, I count homes—50 rows, 10 deep, identical. Where is everybody?

Ah, here they are. Across the canal, a multi-level holiday development rises. An announcer bellows from a speaker somewhere in the middle. More of the same fancy sedans park within inches of each other. With no way around this monstrosity, I stay on the road.

Greenhouses to my left. Chain-link fence and barbed wire surround forests to my right. What happened to the beach? Likya, where are you?

It's only been four hours, but my feet tingle and the asphalt burns through my thick soles. Flip flops? I can walk all day in $4 flip flops, thin as yoga mats—but with a 30-pound pack?

Just after noon, I buy a loaf of warm bread. As it bounces in rhythm with my poles, I cruise down a side street that ends at Mavikent Park, adjacent to the long, white beach. Finike bookends the west end of the bay, making it possible to walk the beach the whole way. A path leads past empty picnic tables to a shady bench facing the beach, the ideal spot for another best damn cheese and tomato sandwich.

No one? Seriously, where is everyone?

As the beach narrows into cliffs, Likya shows up on the hilly asphalt—*Finike 22 kms. Karaöz 8kms.* Okay, maybe 90 minutes. Feet? Can you do this?

Cars packed with families fill the road. With no centre line and no shoulder, I step aside when cars pass. When two cars pass at the same time, I step into the shrubs. Six teenagers on motorbikes weave by. One motorbike backfires and makes me jump. They try to repeat it again and once more. Boys.

My feet have surpassed burning, tenderness now reducing into numbness. Pine trees tower out of the steep slope atop the orange rocky cliffs that freefall into the turquoise below. The left slope is impossible to climb.

I walk on.

I fill up my water—again—at a roadside tap.

I walk on.

"Merhaba! Do you speak English?" I yell across the road to the hiker. My feet envy his heavy-duty sandals.

"A little. I'm from Russia."

"Canada. Is their camping in Karaöz?"

"Not really, not until you get closer to the lighthouse," he says. "Maybe a pansiyon in Karaöz for you? You'll like Karaöz."

After two nights away, I am craving my tent. Wait, here's a beach with perfect camping, even bathrooms, but it's jammed with families barbecuing, kids playing and teenagers doing wheelies on their mopeds. No thanks. I need quiet after today's emotional and physical energy drain. The road splits, and my map shows Likya close to the beach. Road or beach? But what about the cliffs? How do I get around the cliffs?

Stop.

I step off the road, slam my pack into a tree and plunk my butt on a rock. Efes beer cans decorate the shrubs like Christmas ornaments. I sip my water. I scan my map. I review my book—*one last headland before Karaöz* it says.

"Just a little bit longer, feet."

A final downhill drops me in front of a sign with directions to a pansiyon. A left, right, left and I'm here.

"Helllloooo?"

"Likya!" says a man coming out of a house.

"Evet."

"I show you room," he says in English.

In an adjacent building, open rooms display white towels waiting on multi-colour bedspreads. My air-conditioned room has two single beds and a tiled bathroom with shower.

"Evet, ne kadar?"

He mutters in Turkish, shrugs his shoulders and smiles as he looks down. I don't like starting the barter but my feet burn so I push my hand into a pocket to pull out a 20 lira note.

"Oh, small," he says, holding his index finger a centimetre from his thumb.

"Ne kadar?" I ask again.

Uh-oh. My hand spreads over my stomach. Hurry, hurry.

He draws 3-0 on his hand and asks, "Ten more?"

Greyness sinks from the ceiling and closes in from the sides. What's going on?

I give him 40 lira, focusing on the straight tile edges instead of his fast-moving hands digging for change in every pocket. Am I going to faint?

"No problem, later," he says as he hands back a twenty and disappears down the hallway.

I unlace my boots, peel off my socks and whip off my clothes. I'm still so hot. My hand cups my mouth as my head swivels for the bathroom door, but the room spins and erases any direct line to the toilet. I grab the garbage can and sprawl on the strip of carpet. Paleness replaces fire on my soles, but the rawness remains, even a caress is too much. Is this heatstroke? Will ibuprofen help? What else is in my first aid kit? I glance at my pack ten feet away, ten feet too far. The cold tile floor feels good on my feet, but if my feet stay longer than ten seconds, the cold hurts and makes me nauseous.

After a half-hour of switching between cold floor and carpet, I sit up and slide the empty garbage can back into its corner. It's over.

After a shower, a baseball cap and a scarf protect me—I've had enough sun—and a short walk leads me to the beach.

"Merhaba," I say to two men standing by parked motorbikes.

"Merhaba," says one man.

Could I rent a motorbike in Turkey? Ride the coastal highway?

A lone picnic table centres me on the beach. The wind creates chaos of my scarf, and the waves are wild. There's no way I'd swim in there. A man walks beside a dog (is that his dog?) before he leaves on a motorbike, the dog following behind him. In a few minutes, he returns.

"Merhaba," I say and wave.

"You want to write or okay I sit?"

"Thank you for asking. It's okay, please sit."

"Where are you from?"

"Canada. I walk the Likya."

He slides black sleeves over muscular forearms as his beautiful eyes pull me into conversations about dogs, the weather and Al Pacino.

"How many people live in Karaöz?"

"About 250, but in summer, 500."

"Turkish people?

"Yes, German too, I work in restaurant, very busy in summer."

"Yes, always working, me too. I understand that."

"You writing a book?"

"Maybe, about Likya." I flip through my pages and he smiles.

"Ah, so good. What is your job in Canada?"

How do I explain this? Earlier he told me about a swimmer who got into trouble (a riptide I think) but was saved by someone.

"You know the swimmer out there?"

I simulate chest compressions and mouth-to-mouth and he nods. "But not for people, for köpek."

"Ah! For dogs! I love dogs."

"Me too."

"I'm Selçuk."

"I'm Michelle."

"Me-shell, Me-shell, okay."

I like how he says my name. It wasn't until two months ago that I learned, or realized, that my dad said my name differently too. "It's Me-chelle, not Mi-chelle, like Me-chelle, my belle," he said.

"You want to go see?" as he points across the bay.

"How far is it?"

"Three kilometres, along the Likya road."

"Okay. I ride a motorbike too."

"You want to drive? You can drive."

I point to my flip flops.

"When I was younger I drive fast, but now, no need. I drive slow," he says.

"How old are you?" I ask.

"Thirty-two, and you? Oh sorry, no question to ask woman, sorry."

"No, it's okay, I'm 45."

"You look young."

"Teşekkür ederim."

We stop to buy two beer and then putt-putt along at 20 km/h on the rutted dirt road as we chat about his friend who has a tiny house nearby.

"He has six dogs. Do you want to see the dogs?"

"Yes please!"

Black and tan, barking, bouncing puppies greet us.

"They're always tied up?" I ask.

"Sometimes, during the day, if many cars on the road or my friend not here, like now, but later." He mimes puppies running around the yard.

As I get closer, the first puppy backs away, so I kneel down and face away. He walks up and sniffs me, allowing me to scratch him under the chin before he flops over for a belly rub. I say hello to all the pups and their relaxed momma.

"For et? Meat? Or eggs?" I ask, pointing to the free-range chickens.

"Meat."

"Ah, I don't eat meat, vegetarian."

"Oh Me-shell, that is so good. You have good heart. I don't eat meat, but fish, yes. I try not to, but I love fish, especially with a little lemon," he says with a smile and a wink.

He points to a tiny stone house with a chimney. "I love this house. In summer it is hot but house cool. In winter, cold, but house warm. Especially if raining, tink tink tink on roof. I stay here often, quiet small house," he says. "Me-shell, look."

He points to an ant hole. "Big problem, people want want want, but world finish with want want want. Here, many in small house, nature is good, nature is perfect, people not perfect."

We bounce down the driveway, and I rest one hand on his denim hip while holding the bottles with the other. A few minutes down the road, a bench overlooks three fishing boats in the bay.

"Yes?"

"Perfect."

We talk and laugh for the next two hours.

About writing and books:

"I book book book, no TV, nobody in Karaöz book, only me book book book. You write book?"

"Maybe."

"For people?"

"Not sure."

"Ah, maybe only for you."

Kiss him. But what about my baseball cap?

About animals and things that scare us:

I draw a picture of a snake and mime the big one I saw in the rock wall.

"For me, no problem, but scorpion, no like," he says.

I draw a scorpion in a shower, and I take off my flip flop to mime smacking it.

"Big problem, but maybe, Me-shell, next time, no. Next time, maybe—" And sweeps his muscular shoulder and arm wide to mime brushing it away instead.

"Maybe." I draw a picture of a spider and a shark. "Big problem for me."

"Ah, maybe TV make bad, so no TV, I put my TV in my mom's house. Now no problem."

Kiss him. Kiss him. But it's been so long. I feel so awkward.

And about tattoos:

I try to explain my typewriter font *create* tattoo but he doesn't understand. I point to my other script tattoo, "*There are no walls*, my dog taught me this lesson."

"I don't understand."

I draw a picture of a house, point to the walls and then the tattooed word *walls*.

"I understand."

I then point to the tattooed words *no walls* and sweep my arms across the view, "there are no walls."

He smiles and nods.

"It's part of a Rumi poem," I say.

"You know Rumi? I love Rumi." he says with wide, happy, gorgeous eyes.

"Rumi is my favourite poet. They say there is a doorway from heart to heart but what is the use of a door when there are no walls."

We sit in silence and watch the sunset, his heavy arm leans against my leg.

Kiss him. Kiss him. God damn it, kiss him.

"A dog," he says and jumps up.

A small, black dog trots up the road, tongue swaying. He takes our plastic bag and race walks to the taps. He kneels, the dog drinks, and Selçuk waves goodbye as the dog trots off.

"Me-shell, we go?"

On the ride back to the restaurant, both hands grip his lean waist and with each bump, slide around and further forward onto his tight stomach. Inside, I meet his brother, Mehmet, and his mom, who watches TV off to the side. And outside, his dog.

"She's tied?"

"Not everybody likes dogs inside the restaurant, but later." And he mimes her running around.

"How old?"

"I don't know, she come to my house."

"Oh right, a stray dog. What's her name?"

"Bob."

"Bob?"

"Bob Marley. Me-shell, we go?"

We walk the three blocks to my pansiyon while Bob runs and plays.

"Me-shell, I love talking with you, me Turkey, you Canada, but," he points to his head and mine.

"Yes, we click, small world, I'm really glad we met."

"It's because you said hello, when you first passed me on the street. You smiled and said hello."

Now we say goodbye, with a strong hug.

"Me-shell, you go tomorrow?"

I look at my watch, "Hmm, not sure."

DAY 18

Karaöv

A FTER A PAUSE FOR THE MORNING call to prayer, I return to my R-rated dream about Selçuk.

At the beach, I find my beloved sarong folded under the picnic table. I hadn't even noticed I lost it. Write, write, write, all afternoon until Selçuk drives by. Does he see me blushing?

"You want to swim later?" he asks.

"Maybe. I will finish writing, then come for dinner, okay?"

"Okay, many men men men, but no problem."

After a few hours, I walk to the restaurant, and the patio is full of men who stop playing a chips game as I walk down the stairs.

"Merhaba," I say. A few say merhaba back.

"In Turkey, women at home, men men men here," says Selçuk.

As I enjoy a salad and fried potatoes, Selçuk receives a phone call. "My friend has invited me over to say thank you for something. Do you want to come?"

We ride by two-story duplexes with rose bushes and green lawns, balconies above and cement patios below, all similar but not exactly. Could I see myself living here? Too tiny for the long term, but ideal for a week or two, or if working on a writing project, a month or two, or six.

Austrians Stefan and Allie first visited Karaöz 12 years ago and now visit annually. Allie dismisses my hesitation with a hug as everyone shifts to create another seat at the patio table. After introductions—two Turkish men, a French woman, a German man—the conversation deepens.

"We want to thank you," says Stefan as he looks at Selçuk, Kerim and Adnan.

"We are used to the sea," says Allie. "We swam under one wave, then another, then a third, but when we came up, the blue buoy was very far away."

"We were too far away," says Stefan, eyes down.

"We tried to swim, but it was very difficult," Allie says, adding demonstration with both arms. "But we managed to get to the blue buoy and hang on."

"We were pushed under by the waves. We were losing strength," whispers Stefan.

"We started to pray—" says Allie, voice choking, eyes tearing. "And you saw us."

Adnan sits silent, eyes down. He was walking on the empty beach. He saw arms waving, voices shouting. He called Kerim, a lifeguard, who then called Selçuk, a free diver and expert swimmer.

"You swam to us," says Stefan, squeezing Allie's hand.

"You didn't want to let go," says Selçuk, eyes moist, Kerim's too. And mine.

"I didn't, I was so scared," she says, showing the bruises on her forearms where he had tugged.

"You risked your lives to save our own," says Stefan, his voice breaking. "We can't thank you enough, but this meal together is a start."

"Confucious said, you have two lives, and the second one starts when you realize you only have one," says the French woman, in English and Turkish.

At the beach yesterday, Selçuk had told me about a couple that had nearly drowned. He hadn't said that he was actually a part of the rescue. Handsome. A compassionate animal and book lover. And humble.

One arm wraps tight around his waist, the other rests lower, on his thigh. My hips press more into his with each bump on the old roads. Without the barrier of helmets, I get to lean my chest into his wide back, only two thin layers keeping us apart. He smells so good. The four or five blocks back to the restaurant are too short, and yet too long.

The streets are silent as we walk and his dog plays. When we reach the stairs of my pansiyon, we face each other. I'm leaving tomorrow. What more is there to say? He pulls me closer, one hand on my hip, the other slides around the back of my neck. My flattened hands slide across his chest, and settle onto his lower back. Our smiles fade temporarily as our lips meet. Handsome, humble. And a delicious kisser. I wish I was staying in my tent, the privacy of my own tent, rather than a room adjacent to a family's house. Smiles mingle with more kisses and our connection lingers as I tiptoe down the stairs backwards and he strolls down the road with his dog.

DAY 19

Karaöv to Gelidonya

I'T'S ONLY EIGHT KILOMETRES, BUT beer and late nights slow me, muggy weather drenches me. Our goodbye kiss blurs my thinking, so my good friend Likya pulls me along until a voice interrupts.

Kirk, from Melbourne, has travelled the world for two years.

"So, you heard about the Likya Yolu a week ago, and here you are, day one?" I ask.

"Yep, I bought Kate Clow's book and started in Karaöz," he says.

"Do you have camping gear?"

"Nope, just my pack."

Does he know the last three days are totally isolated mountain trails with no pansiyons, no food, no villages, not even shepherds? He doesn't ask and doesn't seem worried, so I keep my fears to myself.

We chat non-stop and walk right off the map. We backtrack. We bushwhack. We laugh. With a stranger, you stay polite. But alone, the searching transitions inward, fast. At the abandoned lighthouse, Kirk continues onwards while I set up camp.

After three hours, the journal closes into silence. Before, I've camped where I can still hear cars, people, the call to prayer, or at least goats. Here? Here, I sit on a silent terrace and face a vague horizon, five islands providing the only depth perception.

Scary?

No.

Uncomfortable?

No.

Lonely?

No.

What is this feeling?

Uh, blank?

Maybe.

Blank.

A foot-wide elevated ledge wraps around the crumbling lighthouse, and the flat cement feels so wonderful under my towel-thin flip flops. With nothing else to do, I walk in circles around the lighthouse and count steps:

One hundred six steps at slow speed.

One hundred sixteen at high speed.

Rapid fire? Ninety-six.

At slow speed again? One hundred six steps.

The counting ends and I circle in silence.

Thoughts loosen.

Clear out.

Blank.

I recline in my camp chair and write more, with tunes. Loud. But at the end of Moby's ambient soundtrack, the setting changes from surrealism back to realism as loneliness sets—look, a dog!

A black and tan shepherd trots up the trail, winds around a tree for the sharp turn up to the olive terrace, and without hesitation, walks up and licks the tear off my cheek.

"Well, you're better than a tissue."

In between pants, her muzzle reaches out and her eyes narrow—one medium brown, one opaque blue, the same colour as the plastic tag in her ear.

"Hi, uh, 171, nice to meet you."

I pour water into a plastic cheese wrapper.

"Whoa, whoa, slow down 171, I can't get more water here."

She takes cheese gently with her lips and tongue as I rub circles into her cheeks. Her panting slows, eyes close. She rolls on her side, stretches forward until her toes flare and sighs.

How long will she hang out? What if she follows me all the way to Antalya? I remember seeing a veterinary clinic. I could change to a pet-friendly hotel until I get the flights figured out. I'll buy a travel crate. What will I name her?

Four hours later, I still sit, well, recline, in my camp chair and twirl 171's ear as she snores.

"I don't know, 171, are you my new dog?"

BARKBARKBARKBARKBARK.

Four hikers pop out of the woods along the trail. With no understanding of Russian, I only get that they are from Moscow and hiking one day, ending tonight. The woman pets 171, and I wave goodbye as the dog drops into line behind them, disappearing back into the trees towards Karaöz.

DAY 20

Gelidonya to Adrasan

WHY DOES LIKYA HIDE? TODAY, through scree, dense forest and open seaside, Likya appears and disappears. I'm starting to understand the games. When Likya first fades away, I lean to the right, step to the left, spin around in the same spot and—Likya! Other times, Likya vanishes, and I'm alone in struggle. Do I want Likya to take my hand and pull me along? Sometimes. But always? No. I don't want a painted yellow line through the forest. Trailfinding is hard. Bushwhacking even harder. But when I reach the clearing, I feel, what? Not sure, exactly. But I know it feels good. But how do I know when to bushwhack or when to lean, step and spin?

Halfway to Adrasan, Helen and Ron say hello. They're on their last day of a ten-day tour before flying back to Holland.

"You are walking alone?" Helen asks.

"Yes."

"Brave."

"Well, I sure wasn't before I started."

"And you have the book too?"

"Yes, I cut it up and taped it to the back of the maps."

"That's smart."

"I was freaking out, so I over prepared. I have GPS on my phone too."

"And what do you do when your battery runs out?"

"I have a solar panel that I strap to my pack as I walk or set up in camp."

"You are prepared."

"I thought I'd need all this equipment. It's nice, but now I know I can do without it."

After hours of grey rocks, beige dirt and muted greens on dry trees, a pink flower greets me at eye-height.

"Oh hello beautiful."

And below, a yellow caterpillar the size of my middle finger, tiny turquoise stars decorate his back, and out of each, a black wisp longer than a supermodel's eyelash.

"Oh, look at you. Will you be as pretty when you're a butterfly?"

He takes the long route and inches along in a straight line, over a rock, along the ground, over another rock. Silly caterpillar.

In early afternoon, a water source appears and rationing ceases. In the shade, I savour a sandwich and my mind drifts. As I start to create a comfort zone of hiking, my inner chatter awakens—*well, it's not Everest*. So when I meet people, I share how scared I was at the start. When they say *brave* or *courageous*, I practice allowing the words in—which silences the inner chatter—but my default to shrug them off is strong.

On the downhill dirt road, a sign—*Maviay Hotel, Walkers Welcome, Cold Beer*. It works. White plastic lounge chairs with yellow and white striped cushions surround the hotel's rectangle pool. Black and brown chickens cluck, scratch and peck at the grass under two hammocks strung between trees with painted trunks.

"Merhaba."

"Merhaba," says Ismet, the owner.

"Pansiyon for bir, ne kadar?"

"Sixty lira" he says.

"Can be smaller?" I ask as I scan the empty restaurant, pool and yard.

"Okay, 50 lira with breakfast only," he says.

"Forty lira, no breakfast?" I ask.

"Okay," he laughs.

"How many kilometres to the village?"

"Beach is 400 metres and village is four kilometres."

I settle into my first floor room with a sliding glass door to the pool. The cold tiles don't hurt. No nausea. All is well.

At the pool, Ismet and I chat as I sip beer. He's a good-looking man, dressed casual in a green and white stripped t-shirt and shorts.

"You have a nice hotel. I like the chickens."

"They are crazy," he says, "they sleep in the trees."

"And the peacock? Does he get outside his pen area?"

"All winter, in summer, he comes to hotel and wakes up guests, so he's there."

"You need a dog."

"I have a dog, Mikey, come see."

At the back of the property sits a dog house, a chain drapes across a cushion inside.

"Puppy puppy puppy," I call out.

Mikey, a black and tan puppy, waddles out and flops onto his back. I throw a piece of tire. Mikey pounces on it and drags it back to me for a repeat. I have extra time, in fact, I have extra days, don't I?

Ismet offers me a drive-through tour of the village. Older stone houses stand adjacent to new stone houses. Then we backtrack through the beach town, with pansiyons and stores and a few people sipping tea at outdoor cafés.

Wanting to relax close to home, I order dinner in the pansiyon dining room. As the only guest, I enjoy salad, peppers and grape leaves stuffed with barley with a ceramic pot of roasted mixed vegetables sprinkled with melted cheese and a basket of bread. My stomach is not in need of this quantity, but I eat it all to avoid the waste.

By 8:30, I'm in bed with a book plucked from the hotel library, about a family who sold everything and moved to Spain.

DAY 21

Adrasan

T HE BAY IS CALM, SHALLOW. And yet I don't swim. Souvenirs dangle from storefronts and stacked lounge chairs wait for company. Head scarves are absent. Only a few tourists return my merhabas.

I buy the usual groceries for today and tomorrow—oranges, apples, cucumbers, tomatoes, cheese, bread and peanuts.

"Merhaba, günaydin," I say to the shop owner.

"Oh, Turkish, good."

"Very little" I say. "Ne kadar?

"*On* and *dört*," he says slowly with a smile. Ten and four.

"Teşekkür ederim," I say as I give him 14 lira. He gives me a lollipop.

I find the Likya trail at the end of the beach area, good to know, and backtrack to the hotel by noon where my pen drags out two hours of writing before my brain melts into a stack of English celebrity magazines. Four hours later, the lounge chair shoves me upright, and I walk across the lawn sipping my first beer. Mikey lies recumbent and motionless, except his tail, which behaves like an erratic drawbridge across his water dish.

Rest. Book. Beer. Beer. Book. Sleep.

DAY 22

Adrasan to Çirali

"IF YOU HAVE ANY PROBLEMS, any at all," says Ismet, "you call me."

"Teşekkür ederim, Ismet," I say as I tuck his business card into my pocket. "And don't forget about Italy."

In a half hour, I meet Likya, but once across the river, the waymarks disappear. Even if GPS shows the trail, I feel more at ease if Likya's present. And then, a Likya billboard—two hip-height cement tubes topped with rock cairns plus dark red arrows pointing right. Got it!

Once in the forest, Likya is an expert guide for six hours. Thunder bellows behind, goat bells ring ahead. After climbing uphill all morning, a clearing showcases a square wooden platform where three park benches hang out and invite me in. You know what? Never throw orange peels off a cliff with the same hand holding the knife.

Likya continues to guide, and my mind loosens back to yesterday. Ismet had shared all about his relationship, his divorce. "I'd like to go to Italy, but I'm alone," he said. "I was scared to come to Turkey alone, but it was either go alone or don't go at all. And I'm really, really glad I came."

I laugh out loud thinking of Anna, the hotel cleaner. She was walking Mikey, and I had pointed to the water, then Mikey. "Yes?" She nodded and plopped him in the shallow end, which only covered his feet. Then she picked him up under the arms like a baby and dipped him in deeper. Mikey had responded to the fun with a round of puppy zoomies in the grass.

I had said to Ismet, "Anna dipped Mikey in the pool."

He shook his head. "Turkish people no like dogs in the pool."

"Uh-oh, did I get them in trouble?"

"No, just Turkish people no understand dogs in the pool," he had said with a smile and a laugh.

A bird screech pulls me back into my footsteps just as a thumb print-size frog hops off the skinny trail and onto a rock, something I would've missed if it wasn't for its movement. Movement creates awareness. One of the reasons why I think long-distance walking can be so enlightening.

More thunder. Longer. But to the right of me. Rain I can handle but a lightning storm?

By mid-morning, the sudden expansive view of the valley from the top of the pass makes me gasp. I don't miss my camera at all. I want to stand in the photograph, absorb the echo of village dogs barking, feel the minimization from the magnitude of the bordering mountains. I drop my pack and because of isolation, strip off my shirt too so air can flow against my back.

"Oh yeah, my apricots!"

"Oh no, my apricots!"

Overlooking a Turkish valley. Eating squished Turkish apricots. In my bra. Well, this is a moment.

Later, I meet David from Florida. His white Columbia long-sleeve shirt looks so fresh compared to my no-longer-white, sweaty t-shirt. He started in Hisarçandir, at the end, and is hiking back to Fethiye.

"Is there a water source the last two days?" I ask. The best person to ask for advice is someone who's done it.

"The first day, no. It shows water, but I never found any. The second day, yes, two spots, lots of water," and shows me on my map.

"What about food or water near Göynük?"

"Yes, there's a restaurant, so lots of food and water," he says and shares no concerns about my solo status.

"Are you doing the whole hike?" I ask.

"I may take buses to skip the boring parts."

"You know, I haven't found any boring parts. It's all so different."

"What about the long beach day into Finike?" he asks.

"I know the book suggests to skip it, but I found that day really powerful," I say.

Soon, I pass two Germans, a couple from England and a woman from South Africa—all day-hiking to Adrasan. Fifteen minutes further along the trail, I meet her husband.

"Well, you must be Chris."

"I am!"

"Your wife said for you to shout out a hello so she knows where you are."

"Okay, I will, thanks," he says. "And you have your heavy bag. You're hiking the whole way?"

"I am."

"Camping? Alone?"

"Yep."

"Wow, what day are you on?"

"Day 22."

"And you do this a lot in Canada then?"

"No, I did one six-day hike and now this."

These supportive little conversations are so appreciated and remind me how much I've confronted my fears. The rest of the way is through thick coniferous trees that block the late morning sunshine. Dark, yet pretty. It feels like hiking in my former local mountains of North Vancouver.

In the early afternoon, the Olympos ruins appear through the trees but instead of crossing the stream and entering the official site, I keep to the free access on my side of the river. A roman bath from 200 BC. A theatre. Sarcophagi. Plants and trees wrap and pierce them, creating the feeling that I'm the first to discover them. At the end lies the beach, where clusters of people swim and lounge directly on the sand. The river narrows to a stream but still too deep and wide to cross with boots so I swap into flip flops. The cold water elevates happy feet into ecstatic feet.

The pebble beach leads to an inward path which leads to the three-block long main street of Çirali. Tour buses, big and small, squeeze into gravel parking lots. Drunken voices boom over music from open café windows. On another holiday, I'd stay and load up on cold beers, but today it's apples, apricots and oranges. Likya leads me along the quiet road, winding past two-story buildings tucked behind gates and hedges, most with pansiyon signs.

Water! I debate turning back but find a young man inside a one-chair hair salon.

"Su var?" I ask and point down the street.

"No," he says and points back to town.

"Su?" and I mime a tap.

"Mosque?"

Ah, perfect, where there's a mosque, there's water.

The mosque tower rises behind the cemetery, and on the side road leading to it, stands a shed the size of a fridge—the water tap.

Likya disappears. Am I on the same road? GPS is blank. What happened? It's 3:30. I've the energy for a simple trail with guidance. But wayfinding? Bushwhacking? No.

"Merhaba, Likya Yolu?" I ask a man standing outside a house.

"Evet."

But where's the red and white?

At the next household I ask again.

"Evet, 100 metres, left," he says in English.

Left? Shouldn't it be right? One hundred metres later, a yellow Likya sign points left for Tekirova—19 kilometres—and points right for Çirali—three kilometres. Seems I've taken a back road which skirts around the town rather than the beach road, so yes, now, it's left. Did I miss Çirali? Are there more than the three blocks? Do I backtrack to the beach for camping? Or go forward and stop at the first available spot?

I choose forward. Twenty minutes in, two women confirm.

"Merhaba. Any place to camp up ahead?"

"Yes, a black sand beach in about an hour would be good."

The narrow seaside path climbs up and offers the view of a tiny bay with black sand. Oh yeah, perfect. During the final 45 minutes descent, I meet John.

"Where you from?" I ask.

"Vancouver, you?"

"Me too!"

John hiked most of the trail but has stayed in Olympos for the last few days, unsure if he'll continue. Although absent of a smile, he says he's enjoyed it. However he only brought summer gear, and after freezing on the first mountain peak, he was unsure about the final mountain climb. John seems depleted, and I'm grateful for only feeling tired. We shake hands goodbye.

A lone German couple wades up to their knees. I drop my pack and wade out to join them. As we chat, a man with a daypack walks from the east and we all wave.

"Do you speak English?" I ask.

"A little, from Russia."

"Ah, Canada."

Mikhail is lean and muscular in nylon shorts and t-shirt, with short brown hair, greying above his ears. He explains through broken English and mime that he's here for three weeks and has walked sections of the trail. Currently he's camping behind the main beach, at a pansiyon that includes meals, bathroom and a shower. We both wave goodbye when the Germans leave.

"I go swimming," he says.

"Me too."

He walks down the beach to change into swim trunks behind a boulder and dives into the sea, swimming out far. I duck into my tent to change. I walk in up to my waist and dive in. The cool temperature soothes every muscle, and the black sand massages my feet. I float. And float. When we get within earshot, Mikhail tells me about sea turtles. I tell him I prefer the tortoises because I'm afraid of things under water. He laughs. While Mikhail swims beyond my comfort zone, I whirl around in the water and float for 20 more minutes before retreating to the beach to wrap up in my sarong. He joins me, staying bare-chested as he dries in the sun. I offer him some of my dinner of apricots and peanuts.

"No, no," he says. I know he knows hikers don't carry a lot of food.

"Yes. Please." He takes a few.

I dry while resting on a boulder, and he stands, arms folded. He knows enough English to chat and tells me about his travels in Turkey (he was in Finike before) and Thailand (I was there too). He talks about another country I don't understand.

"Ee-guh-ip."

"What?"

"Ee-guh-ip. Ee-guh-ip? Ee-guh-ip," as he points to a map on his journal.

My intense laughter prevents me saying the correct pronunciation.

"Ee-guh-ip? Ee-guh-ip?" he says again and again, making me howl.

"Egypt. Oh my goodness, sorry for laughing. It's Egypt."

"E-jipt, okay. E-jipt." We share more laughter.

When he describes his next travel journey, he says, "Yugoslavia" and places his hands together, exploding his fingers in every direction.

"You understand?"

"Oh, I totally understand," I say and start howling all over again.

He sits beside me on the big rock in the sun, close enough that our arms brush whenever we mime. I sneak glances at his handsome face as he shows me his notebook for the Likya Yolu, with handwritten Russian-to-Turkish translation lists in the back, along with map cut outs and highlighted routes. I show him my handwritten English-to-Turkish translation lists in the back of my journal, along with map cut outs and highlighted routes. We practice our Turkish together and add English and Russian too. I show him my Google Translate app on my cell phone and he laughs. He has it too.

I show him my word list:

"Goat, *keçi*," I say.

"Goat?"

"Ba-aa-aa."

He laughs.

"Sheep, *koyun*."

"Sheep?"

"Ba-aa-aaa" I say as I grab a tuft of hair and plunk it on my arm.

"Ah yes, I understand," he says, as he taps my forearm, lingering on the last tap.

It's close to seven. We've chatted for two hours, sitting closer each minute. Great conversation. Handsome man. Loves hiking. The sun sets in an hour, and it's an hour back to Çirali. Do I go with him? Take a day off in Çirali?

"Uh, you have to go," I say.

"Unfortunately, maybe we hike together one day?"

"Maybe."

"It's a small world, maybe we see each other again?" he says.

"I'd really like to."

He puts on his daypack, and we shake hands. He stops shaking and holds both my hands.

"It's a small world," he says.

I squeeze back. Do I have to be the one? I'm always the one to start something. Why can't the guy be the one to start something?

"Goodbye, Mikhail."

"Goodbye, Michelle."

He grabs his trekking poles and walks backwards along the black sand, waving as he walks. I wave back. I watch him climb up the steep cliff trail. He stops walking, turns and looks down at the beach and me. I look up and wave. Shit. Shit. Shit. We pause, just looking at each other for two, three seconds. He waves, I wave. At the crest of the trail, he pauses again. I've been puttering around camp so I'm not staring at him, but I see him out of the corner of my eye. I look up and wave. He waves. He stands still for another three or four seconds. Then he turns and disappears.

I write for the next hour with the waves as the soundtrack and fall into a dream of living in Russia.

DAY 23

Çirali to Tekirova

A S SOON AS ONE EYE QUIVERS, the brutal sun yanks me through the half-zipped tent flap, but the water saves by naked body from overheating in a single splash. I float in a position to watch the top of the ridge, for the hikers I don't want to see and the one man I do. I'm unsure which fulfills more, the having or the longing?

By 9 o'clock, I'm crossing the third black sand beach—*a mainly easy, long route*, says the book—where three men and a woman sit on a blanket.

"Günaydin, çay?" says one man as he sweeps his arms wide to welcome me.

"Evet, lütfen," I say and accept the glass of tea.

"Where are you from?" asks the woman.

"Canada."

"Where is your boyfriend?"

"Uh, Canada."

A rustle behind me makes me swivel—a black and tan head with a dangling tongue pokes out of a bush.

"Ahhh, a Rottweiler!" I yell. "I had a Rottweiler too."

Pasha, a six-month-old Rottweiler who looks like my Monty, is tied to a tree. A 20-pound bag of kibble and a full water dish sit nearby. I kneel and he leans into my thighs. No barking. No licking. No jumping. Just a classic Rotti lean. Pasha's wet fur soaks my pants.

"Oh sorry, he was swimming."

"No problem, I love him!"

I thank them for the tea and turn to face a wide, open meadow. Which way? They all point in one direction. I don't see any signs or a worn path, but I walk in the general direction of their outstretched arms.

One Likya waymark sits on a rock on the dusty roadside, directly in front of another rock with a red painted X. Which one to believe? I decide to get a third opinion, but my phone won't turn on. Hold for 20 seconds. Nope. Thirty seconds. Nope. Forty? That works.

GPS cannot be found.

Shit.

I pass both the Likya waymark and the red X, hoping for a confirmation further down the road. Nothing. But at least, I am on an obvious dirt road. That should lead me out? Up a mountain, around a curve. Up another mountain, around another curve. Ninety more minutes of switchbacks with few trees, sweat drips off my downward forehead and evaporates when it hits the red rocks.

A single tree provides shade so I drop my pack, whip off my shirt and wring it out before hanging it in the sun—benefits to total isolation. My solar panel recharges as I devour an orange. In front of me is the sea and behind me are wide paths carved out of crumbling rock, leading inland over switchbacks.

I reread my book: *the way to Tekirova is mostly downhill...*

"Bullshit."

A descent drops me onto a flat area where the double-track path divides into five unmarked directions. I consult with GPS, which is operational, but doesn't match the way I think the narrative describes. I choose GPS. At the very least, I can back track to Çirali.

A tap appears. Well, not exactly a tap, more like a concrete bathtub with a rigid hose protruding from a metal fixture. For goats? I crank the lever and water blasts like a fire hose straight at my crotch. My inner four-year-old howls. This time, I slowly twist the lever, and a tiny stream blasts out and soaks me again, causing more giggles to erupt.

Seriously, Michelle, move to the right.

Fatigue makes simple actions and simple decisions challenging, which can lead to meltdowns. Or preferably, as in this case, giggle fits.

Up a hill. Down a hill. When the path splits in two, or three, I sneak a peek at GPS for a one-second confirmation (to avoid draining the battery). Although the switchbacks create an erratic red line that jitters across the screen, the orange you-are-here triangle always hovers on it.

In the early afternoon, the first hikers I see are two Turkish men. Up a hill. Down a hill. Trail split. Choose a direction. Sneak a peek at GPS. An hour later, I see two Russian beach-goers.

"Merhaba, how far to Tekirova?" I ask without asking if they speak English first. In my estimation, I'm in the last 30 minutes.

"About two hours."

"Two...hours?"

My forced smile disappears. My shoulders slump. My poles drag. Two more *hours*?

Up a hill, down a hill. Sun cracks my lips. Sweat stings my eyes. Water simmers in my drinking tube. I need to get wet, but this trail teases and drops near the beach before pivoting inland, up and over another headland. Likya abandoned me when I stopped for morning tea and hasn't returned. Grey painted squares appear on rocks sometimes. Is Likya hiding under there? Has the route changed? Is GPS fucking with me?

An hour more, an architectural monstrosity with towers and domes peeks out of the distant trees and would seem more at home in Las Vegas than Turkey.

Finally, the trail leads to an empty beach where I ditch my boots and hobble to the sea through discarded pop cans and whisky bottles. While sore feet recover on an elevated tree trunk, I create a gourmet sandwich with hot bread, hot flattened tomatoes, melted cheese and a cucumber that's almost-a-pickle. Only panini grill lines are missing.

A tall ship with black sails and gold rigging sails into the tiny bay. A pirate ship? It drifts right, and yeah, a skull and cross bones decorate the stern. Three more identical ships sail into the bay, heavy bass dance music and an announcer's voice shouting through loud speakers. Are these waves or reverberations?

Movement at the far end of the beach pulls my eyes from the pirates. Dogs?

Horses. Two horses gallop along the surf and pause to nudge necks before rolling in the sand, eight legs waving in the air. I so want to camp with the horses. But without water or food, I must move on.

The dirt road ends at asphalt. A yellow Likya Yolu sign lies under overgrown bushes. The book says to either catch a bus into town or turn right and *slip between the two holiday villages onto the beach then walk to the centre.* Right it is, of course. I pass Hotel Euphoria, with eight tennis courts and two security guards. Taxis and tour buses line the circular driveway. At the dead end, stands another hotel. A guy cleaning a bus stop says the first market is three kilometres away, three kilometres in soft sand. I decide to backtrack, and pass a street pole with the first red/white Likya waymark I've seen since 9 o'clock this morning.

"Fuck you, Likya," I mutter.

Exhaustion not only makes simple decisions challenging, it makes me cranky. I have enough self-awareness to know I'm cranky but not enough energy, or desire, to stop it. Eventually, I find a market and linger in front of the cooler, deciding on a juice.

"Can I help you?" the clerk asks.

"No thank you."

He stands within inches and stares.

"Can I help you?"

I shake my head as I tuck wayward hair under my baseball cap and brush the dirt from my t-shirt.

"Can I help you?"

As I reach for a juice, I hand him money and don't wait for change or take a seat on his patio.

Bare-chested men in tight shorts walk beside women in tight t-shirts, short shorts and high heels. No fruit, vegetables or bread for sale, anywhere. Signs display only Russian letters and hang above leather shops, fur shops, luggage shops and jewellery shops.

Get me. The fuck. Out of here.

With multiple checks of GPS all day, my battery barely survives. So I rig up the solar battery, winding the cord into my front hip pocket to plug in my cell phone. With no benches along the streets packed with parked cars, I sit on a cement curb and check in with GPS. It's only now I realize that if I only sneak a peek at GPS, it doesn't have a chance to calibrate to my new position, so it always looks like I'm on the trail. All those path splits through the mountains for the last four hours? I don't know what guided me back there, but it wasn't GPS.

After a minute of walking, I pat the left pocket of my pack. No phone. I whip around and look—no phone. Shit. A guy passed me. Was it him? That guy? I spin around again to look for That Guy and my phone hits me in the leg, dangling from the white cord. I didn't (1) scan before leaving a place I've sat and (2) check my pockets to ensure everything is in its rightful place.

Fatigue changes the rules.

The street soon dead-ends at a resort hotel.

"No," says the guard and points back towards town.

"Likya?" I ask. He ignores me.

I backtrack the half hour, as electronic music thumps from behind 12-foot perimeter walls, and arrive back to the main north/south street. I ask pedestrians and shop owners, but they don't know Likya. I'm sinking.

Water.

Food.

Shelter.

I find a market and buy bread, cheese, tomatoes and water—and seriously consider the multiple brands of Russian vodka—and cross the street to sit on a bench overlooking the shallow river littered with pop bottles and beer cans and a rainbow of plastic.

After I saturate, I pack my food and move onwards and spot a yellow sign pointing right—*Phaselis 3kms.*

Oh thank god.

I turn right—the book talks about a flight of stairs soon after—and there they are, there they are!

I climb the stairs, and a faded white/red Likya waymark appears on a pole, but a man on the street says it isn't the Likya, and the road only goes to a hotel. I can't do another dead end. GPS still shows the erratic red line of the mountain switchbacks.

I show him my map, but he directs me back to the main road and, I think, to the highway to catch a bus. I try to explain the Likya Yolu hike, a hike without buses. He asks a man driving a tractor. No help. I walk him back to the yellow Likya sign on the main road. He nods and crosses the street to ask a shop owner. No help. He asks four young men standing on the road who also indicate the highway and a bus.

"No there, can't walk" says the one who speaks minimal English.

I want to appreciate their help. I want to be grateful for him asking so many strangers in an attempt to help me.

"Boya boya boya," I say. Hardly a gesture of gratitude but it's all I got.

I sit on the curb and wait for a bright idea. I scan left and spot a red/white Likya paint splotch on a pole. Makes NO sense. I reread the narrative: *just beyond a flight of steps rises to a G6 road. Follow this to a junction and turn right, at the next junction, turn left.* Wait. Maybe it means to pass the stairs, not climb the stairs? At this point, I need baby step directions, ultra clear guidance. A yellow painted line. I cross the road but instead of climbing the stairs, I pass them and follow the side road which soon comes to a junction. I go straight, and it feels like I'm going the right way but still no Likya. Likya, where are you? Help me! As I stand on the side of the road, a green truck pulls over.

"Do you need help?" she asks.

"Do you know the Likya Yolu?"

"Yes."

"Am I on it?"

"Yes."

"Oh thank god."

"Do you want a ride?" she asks.

"Where are you going?"

"Towards Phaselis, it's only a few kilometres."

"Okay, yes please."

I climb in and Meryem says she's heading to a camp I've read about, although internet comments say it's expensive.

"Do you work there?"

"I live there and help my friends, the owners."

In minutes, we arrive and pass a sign: *Köpek Var.* Dogs Here.

"That's cool, and do they have beer?" I ask.

"Oh yes."

"Well, okay, then."

An overweight golden retriever barks as I get closer to the entrance. I kneel and turn backwards but my calming signals don't work. I pass him in an arc but he growls and snarls as he pulls himself from his lounge position.

She hands me a cold Efes beer. "Go relax, and I'll sign you in later."

I set my pack against a picnic table in the yard and pull out my journal, pausing first to pet the sleeping cat curled on a wooden chair. A group of five women in white, flowing cotton pants and long-sleeve shirts and soft pastel scarves, float by like banshees. A young man in capri pants and bright striped t-shirt walks arm in arm with a female twin, neither acknowledging my smile. Can they feel my cranky aura? A group of men and women huddle around the other picnic table speaking French, yoga mats resting at their feet. I look at my dirty, sweat-stained t-shirt and chuckle as I gulp my beer. Have I crashed a private yoga party?

Meryem explains the current camping prices, and it's more than I've paid previously for a clean, private, pansiyon room, but I'm looking forward to the vegetarian buffet at 7 o'clock. I set up my tent under a tree and shower in an outdoor hut. Then I wash my clothes and string them up on a clothesline under my tree.

After my attempts to start conversations with my camping neighbours are ignored, I give up and explore the forest. Oh look, a beach. I could've walked ten minutes more and camped in the sand. Alone. For free. And I could have eaten dinner at 5 o'clock and been in bed by 7 o'clock. I don't fit in here. I don't want to be here. Why am I here? Why didn't I just thank her for the ride and continue on to the beach? Did I feel obligated to stay because I got a ride for ten minutes? Exhaustion blurs clarity and then I find myself where I don't want to be.

Dinner buffet is lovely though, well, the food anyways: broccoli and cauliflower salad, lentil salad, barley salad, carrot and herb salad, plus chick pea humus, stuffed peppers, roasted vegetables, bread.

"Hi! May I join you all?" I ask one table.

"No, this seat is taken," he says.

"Hi, may I sit here?" I ask another table as I point to the empty chair.

"Sure."

"Great, thanks."

"We're all just leaving."

I eat in silence as the room swirls in white cotton. I fill another plate, and the golden retriever snarls whenever I walk by.

DAY 24

Tekirova to Roman Bridge

M Y TENT BROKE. I DID HEAR a *pop* during the night but thought a pine cone had bounced off a tent pole. But this morning, the foot end slopes strangely, the poles disconnected. I pull them apart and the stretchy inner cord is still intact, but the poles won't reconnect, one end won't slip over the other.

I don't understand.

I bang the ends together, one, twice. No go.

WHY NOT?

I yank apart two other poles to compare. The red aluminum pole slips off the silver aluminum inner lining of another pole. I look again at the broken poles. No exposed silver. I look inside each pole. The silver aluminum tip has snapped off and is stuck inside, so now there's no way for the poles to connect together. I take everything out of my tent and it collapses. Now what? Can I sleep in a broken tent? Might work. But not if it rains. Tape it? Will that hold for five more nights?

"Fuuu-ck."

I'm already exhausted due to repeated bathroom visits all night and a disruptive dream where I cancelled a road trip because I couldn't zip my coat and the four-door car only had three. Should I bail? After all, my tent broke. Everyone will understand.

I snatch my clothes off the line and shutter as they press against my skin. Why didn't I hang them inside as always? I think about my night, and now add grumpy dogs, broken tent and wet clothes. Oh, and diarrhea.

No sign of the Cotton Crowd, but the golden retriever barks non-stop, switching to a growl, snarl and lunges when I trespass through his comfort zone of 15 feet.

"Oh yeah? Fuck you too."

I find my way out of the compound and across the river. The book says *walk north along the beach, on a G5 tractor track ... follow the track away from the sea...the track brings you out at the gated entrance to Phaselis.* I trudge along the sand but the beach ends at a steep headland. There's no way around it and no tractor track inland. I backtrack across the beach where a dozen members of the Cotton Crowd sit in a circle around a gong. Silent meditation?

Wait.

"Ha-ha-ha-haaaaaa," they chant in unison. "Ha-ha-ha-haaaaaa."

I walk to the mountain, slower this time, looking up, looking down. No trail.

I backtrack by the Cotton Crowd a second time.

"Ha-ha-ha-haaaaaa. Ha-ha-ha-haaaaaa."

"C'mon Likya, help me get the hell out of here."

I backtrack a third time, still no Likya signs. One man leaves the group and walks to a bike against a tree.

"Merhaba, do you speak English?" I ask.

"A little."

"Do you know the Likya Yolu?"

"I've heard of it, but don't know where it is."

"What about Phaselis?"

"That's two bays over, by the boats, some walk around, some go up and over."

"Jeepers, that just doesn't make sense," I say. "But uh, okay, thank you."

I slog back to the mountain for the fourth time. With a high tide, there's no way around the headland so I bushwhack up and over.

"Ha-ha-ha-haaaa. Ha-ha-ha-haaaa."

I tumble down the headland, which blocks the taunting, and into the second bay and through a wire fence. Wait, doesn't the book mention a wire fence? But a wire gate is supposed to be after Phaselis. Did I already pass the ruins? I couldn't have. Did I? I blend the narrative with bushwhacking over two more headlands, following the beaches and arrive at the entrance to Phaselis. How is this possible? Am I missing some of the book? Did I not cut and paste this whole section? I search for red/white Likya signs. Nothing.

There!

No, just a Coke bottle.

At the Phaselis ruins entrance, I buy two juices for twice a village market price. Juice Guy doesn't know the Likya Yolu, neither does the woman hosing the patio.

With no Likya waymarks, no obvious trails and missing written directions, I ask GPS—*go left*. I backtrack to a pebble beach. Yes! The narrative says something about a pebble beach. But now GPS says *go right*, I shuffle right, *go left*, and I inch back. *Go right*. I ram GPS headfirst into my hip pocket.

Back at the road, I climb a goat path, and a red painted line appears on a rock. Did they run out of white paint? A few more red lines entice me forward into a painted blue smiley face. Is that confirmation of the right way or reminder to suck it up and smile?

"I don't feel like smiling, Smiley," I say as both poles drag in one hand.

The book mentions a main road, what if I get to it and a dolmuş drives by right at that moment?

There won't be a book if I bail.

It's not about the book.

I start hoping to get further lost. Oh look, now I'm really lost. Taxi?

More red lines and red arrows—red arrows now? Sure, why not? But wait, is that the sound of cars? The map shows a highway crossing and the books says *to meet the main road and walk right for about 100 metres* before crossing the road.

It's not busy, but the buses and cars race along. It doesn't seem right that I have to run across two lanes, hop a centre barrier and dart across another two lanes. I revive GPS, the first time since chasing red arrows for half-hour, and I'm waaay off. Again. I backtrack and follow another direction. But it doesn't feel right— no waymarks, no red arrows, and why am I going northwest when I think I want to go northeast? Turn off, turn on, recalibrate. Repeat. Why do I continue to listen to GPS when I know it's not helping?

I know my attitude is pitiful, but I can't recover. And I don't even care. I attempt a shift with a rampage of gratitude, but even *I'm grateful to be in Turkey* seems like a lie right now. No point in continuing fake gratitude.

What's going on? Am I supposed to stop? Or push through? How do I know when to quit and when to persevere? I've been asking Likya for signs all morning and all I get are half red stripes and smiley faces.

Likya, where are you?

I pass through another wire fence, and I'm unsure if this is a new wire fence or the one the book mentions earlier. My hiking vortex is now three hours. The whole day was estimated to be six-and-a-half hours, but I'm only a quarter the way on the map.

At 10 o'clock, a red/white Likya waymark.

Then nothing.

Did I hallucinate that?

I climb up one headland and down another. I want to take a break and get wet in this secluded bay, but six men lounge on a power boat close to shore. Nope.

The next bay hosts a dozen Turkish families picnicking. I say merhaba to everyone as I step around their blankets and everyone says merhaba back.

Butts wag, ears flap and tongues loll as a Rottweiler-shepherd and a Kangal-cross run towards me. Well, that's more like it! Both weave around my legs and lick my ankles, and I fall in love instantly. No collars, no ear tags either. Uncounted strays. Uh-oh, they're following me. No, no, it'll be a highway! The dirt road meanders out of the beach area, and a highway comes into view. It looks like four lanes divided, with an off-ramp joining the dirt road to the beach. The Rottweiler-shepherd hangs close while the Kangal-cross rests flat and motionless on the tiny shoulder of the off-ramp.

"That's what I'm afraid of."

A log under a tree invites me to sit, and I slice up an orange. Make that two. The Rottweiler-shepherd watches, so I throw a piece of cucumber. He sniffs but doesn't eat it. No? I divide the last of my cheese into three pieces, but I won't share right now for fear they'll follow the Cheese Lady across the highway.

The dogs do follow as I explore the tunnel underneath the overpass. "No! NO!" They flinch for a second but keep coming so I stomp in their direction—"Hu-yaaa! HU-YAAA!"

They shrink back. My chest tightens.

"I'm so sorry, it's for your own good. I'm sorry."

In the tunnel, the off-ramp amplifies the traffic noise and speed—zshooom, zshooom, zshooom. I lean out, but there's no way to see the cars approach around the sharp curve of the off-ramp. Maybe I can time it based on sound? I could practice without my pack? Images of horrific motor vehicle investigations in the past stop this thinking, and I retreat to the lunch log.

What should I do? Why am I feeling so on my own? Where's Likya? Tears form and I dab them with my sweaty handkerchief. I feel low. Wobbly. The dogs lounge on shaded rocks. I didn't want to yell. It's not right that these lovely dogs have to struggle for water, food, shelter, companionship, when other dogs live extravagant lives. My ribs squeeze tighter.

Wait. Is this THE "main road"? The *meet the main road and walk right for about 100 metres before crossing the road* "main road"? I hoist my pack and hide the cheese deep into a rock crevice. Within minutes, the dogs sniff out the cheese and run towards me and ahead up the ramp. No! No, dogs! Go back! Back! It's dangerous! I call them over as I step off the highway, but they ignore me, continuing to explore litter. I yell. I stomp. "Hu-yaaa! HU-YAAA!" But instead of retreating to the shoulder, they jump out into the road—Honk! Honk! I shade my peripheral vision with my cell phone. I would help the dogs, of course, but I don't want to see it happen. But the dogs aren't hit, and together they run down an off-ramp that joins a driveway of a hotel and straight to people who linger at the gate. At the split in the highway, I run across and walk back towards the overpass until—a Likya signpost! I look back, no dogs. Yes!

Under my boots, sharp rocks mimic marbles as I scale the steep dirt road. In full sun, sweat pours down my back and chest within minutes. Poles drag.

And then one too many marbles. I fall to my knees and pitch forward onto my elbows and hands. And tears explode from a depth greater than physical pain.

"I didn't want to yell at them. I was trying to help, to keep them safe."

"I'm a good person, I showed up, I'm doing it, and it started easy, but now it's hard. And I'm tired. So tired. And thirsty. I can do it, I will do it, but all the backtracking, the getting lost."

"Why are you so hard on me?"

"I've asked for the signs but you're not showing me the way. Why am I alone in this? I don't want to be alone. But I'm here. I'm doing my bit."

"I've asked for help. Where are you? Help me. Please."

My body heaves as I wail into my handkerchief, face down in the dirt. Fifteen seconds, 30 seconds.

I inhale deep and exhale long as I wipe my face. Then, I dust off my knees, wrap each hand around a pole and hike up the hill.

After an hour of up and down, I arrive at a village. Is this Asağikuzdere? No one to ask. I spot a Likya sign, and five minutes later, I check GPS which says I'm off the trail. I backtrack, locate another Likya waymark, then no more. I do this sequence three times. Four times? I'm no longer counting.

I invite conversation with a couple biking around the town. They're from Luxembourg and retired to Kaş but found after a while, "the restaurants play the same songs, you now? So we rent apartments elsewhere for the summer so we can explore."

I crawl back into the woods where the hiking vortex starts again. A severed manikin head stares from a fence post and creates a giggle. "Feeling a little lost? Yeah, me too." The forest drops me onto asphalt and into a rickety bus stop. Okay, maybe I won't quit. Maybe I just need to stop and regroup. Another break. Why not? I have an extra day. A day off in a pansiyon. A shower. A hot shower. No decisions to make. A complete mind break. Maybe dinner. Ooh, yes! A pansiyon with dinner! With a plan in place, I float down the road as I imagine roasted vegetables, cold beer, English newspapers and chit-chat with nice people. People! No navigating. No decisions. No thinking, period. Blank mind. Oh yeah, I'm staying in whatever town this is for the night. Definitely.

My feet wince on the hot pavement. But it's downhill, and I bounce along dreaming of fluffy towels. Where is everyone? Fences border empty yards. Metal bars protect lower windows on houses, the mosque too. A massive dog lunges towards an open gate. I leap onto the far sidewalk to flatten against the building, but his chain yanks him back. In the next yard a dog leaps at the top of a spiked fence and further down, a third growls and barks and snorts behind a dense hedge. At least I think it's a dog. I slither off the wall and into an open doorway, a market, and select an iced tea. The clerk chats on a cell phone, so I silently place coins on the metal counter. He counts out change and throws it on the counter—clang! clang!—without eye contact or a break in his conversation.

As I fish for my coins, I whisper, "Pansiyon var?" and point down the road. He waves me off. Is that a yes?

A woman pushes a stroller.

"Pansiyon var?" She nods.

I ask the third man on the street, "Pansiyon var?"

He points to a two-story building with balconies.

"Evet?"

"Evet."

There's no pansiyon sign but I knock on the heavy wooden door that doesn't quite fill its frame. No answer. I push the door open. It's dark. Five pairs of shabby shoes form a pile in the middle of the hallway, a staircase leads to more darkness. I step inside. No lights come on.

"Merhaba?" I whisper.

No answer.

It looks lived in, but no current life. Definitely no fluffy towels. I step back outside and close the door.

Another man on the street says, "pansiyon, no, apartment, evet."

"Pansiyon var?"

"No."

"No pansiyons?"

"No."

Not a single pansiyon in this town? So many houses and no pansiyons? Did I misunderstand?

Depletion creeps in.

A water tap in a tiny pie-slice of a green space invites me over. I collapse onto the one bench as a dolmuş rumbles by. Then a taxi. Another dolmuş. My hand jingles coins in my pocket. Everyone will understand. But will I? With all the unwelcome events, it's clear I'm not supposed to be in this village, but what's next? Is there a next?

I unlace my boots and slip free. My feet ooze beyond my flip flops as I stand to fill water. I unwrap my bread. I nibble. And fail to notice the next 40 minutes.

And then, something makes me stuff my feet back into their boots and peel myself off the bench. I hobble back to the market, pass the three dogs, pass the bus stop and onwards to the Roman Bridge.

The Kemer Gorge swallows me. To the left, its grey walls soar, the sun soars higher. To the right, a vertical drop to the river. Each minute, a car negotiates the steep and cracking asphalt road. I feel microscopic. My head droops and my eyes rest on the rhythmic shuffle. Click-clack-scuff.

Up. And up.

I pass a park where families picnic next to the river. Can I camp there? No. What about the one-car pull-outs on the side of the road? *Don't be silly.*

Up. And up.

A sign for a river-side café pulls me across the road for a peek over the edge. A deck hangs over the edge of a natural pool of river water. Wait, the book mentions a tiny café by the Roman Bridge where you can dip your feet in the river. My vision drops under the entrance crossing, and the framework is stone, like an ancient stone bridge. A Roman Bridge.

I'm here.

People fill every table. I'm hot, sweaty, and no idea how smelly. Where will I put my backpack? My dirty boots? Across the jumbled back parking lot, a picnic table. I can only sit, not sure what to do, or not able to do what's next. Some cars leave, some people leave by walking up the back lot and over a hill to the right. What's up there? A couple walks down the hill.

"Merhaba, do you speak English?"

"A little."

"What's there?" I ask and point to the hill.

"The river."

"Is there a flat space to camp?"

"Yes, you can camp."

"Teşekkür ederim."

I duck into the outdoor bathroom and change my clothes, switch to flip flops and semi-wash my face using the outdoor sink. My knees and quadriceps survive the steep entrance stairs and—all the customers are gone. Just a bunch of men building a second deck over the water.

A smiley young man welcomes me, "Merhaba."

"Merhaba, bira, lütfen."

I choose a picnic table, tuck my pack in the nook between the table and the river boulders, pour my Efes into a glass and point to the metal stairs leading down to the water.

"Evet," he says and smiles.

As I cool my feet in the frigid river, my open journal waits. But I've got nothing, can't do nothing, but watch the men build a deck.

The women behind the bar also watch and smile. All the men smile despite working in the hot sun. An older man can't start a chainsaw, so a young man comes up and starts it in one try. Turkish erupts along with laughter. The older man rustles the younger man's hair. The deck continues to grow as I snack on bread and a salad with lemon and salt—oh salt, how I've missed you.

About 7 o'clock, I bring along a beer and scout out a flat, sandy campsite between an elevated log and a stream, an offshoot from the main river. Oh right, my broken tent. I tie a length of parachute cord to the centre cross bar and pull—the tent uprights like a ship in a bottle—and then quadruple wrap the cord around a large river rock. Yes!

The elevated log lies two feet off the ground. I sip my beer and swing my feet as if on a dock. Then I lie flat on my back, like a gymnast on a balance beam. My arms dangle outward as I stare up at the darkening sky as John Lennon's "God" opens the music shuffle.

DAY 25

Roman Bridge

DREAMS CONTINUE UNTIL SEVEN, then I flip open the tent doors and watch the shadows shorten on the stream rocks. At 9 o'clock, the tent swaps from chilly to blistering, and I crawl out to stretch, brush, floss and slice up two oranges.

My clothes come back to life in the river and dry while spread across a boulder. Solar panels recharge there too. After I triple-wrap and submerge my cheese, all chores are done except writing. But for now, it's rest time. Feet chill in the water as it rushes for the coast. Leaves flutter and bounce when birds take-off. No navigation. No decisions. No worries. Blank.

At lunch, I return to the restaurant and order the salad, and bread for dipping, again. Tourists old and young enjoy their meals downstairs while I seek quiet under the trees on the deck above. I write for four hours while the men work on the deck. I love watching men build stuff. I feel good. My attitude is good. You definitely have to recharge yourself first, in order to give out, whether it's physically (hiking), mentally (navigating) or emotionally (saying merhaba).

Back at the river, I filter three litres of water, pack up my sun-dried clothes and re-organize my pack. The submerged cheese is a little waterlogged, so I squeeze it with my sarong. That little sarong does everything. Thank you, sarong.

Back for a final visit at dinner, the men are still working. They've built the sides and the gates on the second deck and now work on the roof of the first deck. I order a *gözleme*, a flat bread stuffed with potatoes, cheese and spinach and another for lunch/dinner tomorrow. Even as an unrecognizable mash of mush, it'll be tasty.

As I walk back to camp, dark clouds move in, so does unease. GPS won't locate a satellite, and the battery drains seven percent with all the attempts. I reread the route for tomorrow, Section 25b: *The route is not easy; in one place you cross a scree slide and in two places you have to cross by first hugging the cliff on the left, then a stream to bypass landslides.* And simmering anxiety makes me read further for the last few days, Sections 26 and 27: *Your tough and steep last two days of walking has no supplies. You climb from sea level to 1,500 metres and the path is mostly rocky and difficult to find. Water is scarce and unreliable. The route goes through totally deserted forest, between sheer cliffs. Read the Introduction to Mountain Strategy.*

So, yes, of course I reread the Mountain Strategy: *We suggest that you don't walk mountain sections 19, 24a and 27, alone.* I thought about Section 19 and how I stood at the beginning of the mountain climb above Alakilise and turned around, instead taking the bus into Finike. Am I ready this time? Section 24a is up and over Tahtali Daği, and instead I chose the lower beach route and hit upon my hiking vortex. *Mobile phones may not work and from October to June, the mountains are totally deserted. There are areas of sudden heavy rain or thunderstorms so you should check the weather forecast before starting. Lightning is potentially dangerous on exposed ridges or high passes; if in doubt, descend before starting.* I manage to stop reading, and stuff the book in my pack. One last check, nope, GPS still can't find me.

I lie on the log for 45 minutes before bed, half-listening to Coldplay and half-listening to restless thoughts.

DAY 26

Roman Bridge to (Almost) Göynük Yayla

CLARITY TRANSFORMS A ROUTINE morning. As I dismantle the tent, an outside voice comes in, or an inside voice goes out, and announces: *it's not about you.* Clear. Strong. Definite.

I look up into the trees as swirling thoughts rush in and instantly make sense.

We're of the same. Trees grow, trees sway, trees fall. It's not about the tree. The bad moments, the challenging times—none are personal, it's beyond me. Only something bigger than me, *knows.* It's like the dogs on the highway, they didn't know the big picture, the reason why I stomped and yelled. It's not hardship, it's love. They are loved. I am loved.

An extraordinary sense of belonging swarms my heart as tears overflow.

Why all my recent challenges on the trail? Do I have to know why? Trust is hard, and yet easier.

Why Turkey? I didn't have an answer then, and I don't have an answer now. Well, I don't have an answer to verbalize, but I have a *knowing,* a knowing I needed to come. It might make sense later. Or not. But, I *know* now I don't have to make sense of it, to understand it. I don't have to search for the answer because it's not about me. If it's not about me, how can I find the answer? To let go of seeking is hard, yet easier.

Any questions and hesitations I've had about the next few days, vanish. I *know* I'll be okay. Something's got my back. I'm not alone.

Likya waymarks glow, and when they do disappear, I *know* the way, and the way becomes clearer and easier, even as I scramble across the landslide. My mind swirls outward and inward. The trees, sometimes they die, or at least the leaves die, but it's not about the tree being a good tree or a bad tree. It's only a tree. One small part of Mother Earth. A necessary, needed, part. By simply existing, that tree matters.

To trust doesn't mean to not prepare—I brought maps, GPS and water—but to trust whatever happens, happens. If days get hard, if I start bushwhacking, maybe I'm off the path and need to get back on. But if I'm on the path, yet still bushwhacking, then perhaps it's for Something Greater. Somebody else in the circle. Struggle and pain happen, will always happen. Struggle and pain are necessary. But joy and love will always happen too, joy and love are necessary.

My footsteps lighten.

"Likya Yolu, good morning, günaydin," I say to each waymark.

If Likya is big, I YELL. If Likya is small, I whisper.

If Likya sneaks up, it's rapid fire:

"AhLikyaYoluGoodMorningGünaydin."

Every. Single. One.

"Likya Yolu, thank you, I'm grateful, for your guidance, for you."

My heart's fullness can't help but spill over. It's not about building rock cairns so you'll feel good, it's about feeling joyful, in gratitude first, and then you can't help but build rock cairns—and I've been building them all day.

The path follows a stream lined with bright leafy trees and white boulders. Frogs cheer me on like sideline spectators: *do-it-do-it, do-it-do-it*. A rustle in the bushes startles me—a rabbit, wait, two rabbits!

"Are you telling me to speed up or slow down, rabbit?"

Where are the tortoises?

And the signs keep coming. By 10:30am, a mosque's white and blue tower rises above the green hills. Am I getting close to Göynük Yayla already? My shadow stretches forward on the dirt—poles, backpack, sleeping pad. Hiker girl.

Now when Likya appears, I blow kisses, and when Likya's within arm's reach, I kiss my fingertips and rest them on the red and white paint for a moment. If it's not about me, when challenges happen, then it's not about me when the good happens either. Refusing the gifts, the good, the generosity, is like deliberately turning my head away from the Likya waymarks. They're here, they're giving me the gift of guidance. When the gifts come in whatever form, it's not selfish to accept them. Say yes. Allow them in. Because other days, they'll go, they'll disappear and be replaced with struggle. But I *know* now that they'll be back again. And when they do, welcome them, receive them in gratitude. Circular flow—give, receive, receive, give. The circle is bigger than me, so by me receiving, allowing in the good, the whole circle benefits too.

Around a bend, a heavy village woman blocks the trail, one scarf covers her head, a second covers her nose and mouth, and in her right hand—a foot-long machete. The bushes shake and a chunk of wood falls onto the trail, and she picks it up, strips it of leaves and throws it behind her.

"Uh, merhaba," I say.

"Merhaba! Likya!" she says and giggles.

"Evet, Likya. Firewood?" I ask and cup one hand to mimic a soup pot, and wiggle fingers underneath to mimic fire.

"Evet," she says, and copies my soup pot and fire, giggling.

A sign for a hotel points left, but the trail goes right, so I do too, and meet Alex from Sherbrooke, Quebec, looking all fresh and clean on his second day.

"Did you hike the mountain or beach route?" he asks.

"I'm a water girl, so the beach route," I say.

"How's it been?"

"Well, that day was pretty powerful. The whole hike's been great, well, except for a few days ago, but that could be timing, being the third week," I say. "But today's been, uh, powerful again."

By lunch time, houses appear and arrows point up a driveway, into a yard. Wait, is this the trail or purposely re-directed waymarks?

"Hello," a man says.

"Merhaba"

"Restaurant or Likya Yolu?" he asks.

"Both."

Teoman's orange and black camouflage shorts hang on his lean hips, his short hair the same silver as the military dog tags hanging against his smooth, tanned chest. I follow him to a vine covered patio with plastic tables and chairs where Hazal sits, her exposed short grey hair matches her shirt and slacks. As I sip my two juices, we chat for a half-hour despite their minimal English and my minimal Turkish.

Hazal is from Istanbul, met her husband in Antalya and now lives here, her husband's village. Teoman helps out in the kitchen-turned-restaurant. He's not Turkish, but I can't understand where he's from. I point to the tattoo on his shoulder.

"Military," he says, abdominal muscles lean and flat, even when sitting.

I practice Turkish as we talk and draw about weather, names of the months, numbers one through 20 plus snakes and scorpions, and our laughter escalates with my mosque drawing.

"Cami," I say.

They don't understand. How can I pronounce four letters wrong?

"Internet?" they ask.

"Internet? What? No."

"TV?"

"No, it's not a satellite dish. It's the flag, the crescent on your flag."

I draw a church with a cross for comparison.

"Internet?"

A faint call to prayer interrupts our giggles.

"Evet," as I point to the sky. "Cami."

"Ah! Cami."

"Cami," I repeat. Isn't this what I'm saying?

Teoman draws a mosque, okay, slightly better but almost identical. As he walks away laughing, I point to his drawing, then to mine and shrug. What? That's what I drew too.

"Hey, Michelle!"

I look up and snap my right hand out to catch the orange whizzing across the courtyard – *thwack*.

"Thanks, Teoman."

Across the grass, an A-frame ladder straddles the wire fence. My gratitude continues as every, single waymark radiates off rocks and trees. No GPS needed.

Finally, the deep canyon. And so many possible campsites with feet-in-the-water, body-in-water, opportunities. I am ready to stop, preferring to camp in the canyon before the trail dips back into the forest, but Teoman is here. He ran passed me 20 minutes earlier, but now in the canyon, he sprawls across a sunlit rock. I'm not sure why this canyon feels more isolated than other isolated areas, but it just doesn't feel right here. Is it the canyon? Or is it him?

I wave and pass, as if I'm hiking onwards to the forest. Once the canyon's massive river boulders obscure me, I drop my pack and scout, finding a flat area against the canyon wall with a small floral tree to anchor my broken tent. Once in my swimsuit, I slip into a river pool with a tiny waterfall.

When Teoman peeks around a boulder, I cut short my outdoor shower and wrap my sarong around me as I dry in the sunshine. We chat more about Likya Yolu, maps, my tent and Turkish food. He's friendly and seems interested in conversation. He's impressed with my solo hiking and offers a shoulder massage. An outdoor shower and now a shoulder rub? I hesitate initially but invite him to sit beside me. As strong fingers push and pull, he tells me about his military life. He's been in Turkey either nine months or since 2012. His dad and brother were killed by Russian soldiers. He has since fought in Bosnia, Iraq and most recently, Syria. He shows me stab wounds in his palm and torso. I want to know more. I want to learn what I don't understand.

He reaches around and rests his hand on my knee.

"No," I say and lift it off.

He laughs and holds up both hands—*sorry, sorry*.

I stand up, walk away, and crawl into my tent. Fuck. I want to talk more with Teoman, I want to know his story. Will he understand that's all I want? I hide my skin with pants and a long-sleeve shirt and re-emerge.

We chat about life in Canada, life in Turkey. He says he's 42, I say I'm 45. He shows me his ring with an Arabic symbol.

"They call us terrorists but no, not terrorists."

Terrorist? I think back to Paddy, a man I met in a bar in Northern Ireland. He told me he spent five-and-a-half years in prison—I didn't ask what for—after his parents were killed by the British military. I didn't tell him I was a police officer. I didn't tell him much, but I listened. I listened late into the night and learned his story.

He reaches out and strokes my hair.

"Hayir, arkadaş," I say. "No, friends."

"Sorry, sorry," he says and shrugs.

I retreat to my tent to gather dinner, which I cut up with my Swiss Army Knife, then snap it closed and keep nearby in my pant pocket. Does he not realize that I'm in an isolated canyon? That it'd have to be on my terms? That if he wasn't so pushy, it might've actually happened? I know I said before that I didn't always want to be the one to start something but now I've been shown the alternative and I don't like it. Not here. I change the subject.

I point to the tiny dolphin and blue eye bead pinned to his watch strap.

"Amulet," he says. He unpins it and hands it to me. I admire it closer and hand it back, but he refuses it.

"In Canada, Teoman" as he points to his chest.

"Oh, I'll never forget you."

We chat about dogs, marriages and holiday flings—he doesn't want me to regret not sleeping with him when I turn a hundred and reminisce about my life. I shake my head and roll my eyes.

When I stand up, he stands up, faces me, grips my shoulders and pulls me closer, smiling. I resist. He pulls harder. To block him, I put my forearm against his neck, push in hard, before sliding it up to bang him in the chin.

"Fuuuck. Off."

He drops his hands and smiles. I want him to go. Screw his story. But he sits down, so I change tactics. I show him a photo on my cell phone of me shooting an MP5 submachine gun at the police academy.

"Me."

"You?" he says, raising his eyebrows.

"Yeah. Me."

He touches my arm again, so I stand up and thrust out my hand—a goodbye handshake. Go, please go. He leans in for a hug, but I deflect with a definitive handshake.

"Güle güle," I say.

He holds my hand for five seconds, and then he's gone.

I crawl into my sleeping bag and zip it up tight. As thunder booms overhead and light rain bounces against my tent roof, I hold my pen to a blank page, unable to write.

Ten minutes later, an echo ricochets down between the canyon walls, "Miiiiichelllllle. Gooooodbyyyye."

DAY 27

(Half-way to) Göynük to (Near) Hisarçandir

PINK FLOWERS LET GO AND EASE into the wind. Water accelerates and banks around boulders like a freeform rollercoaster. Amphibian cheerleaders provide the soundtrack—do-it-do-it, do-it-do-it—as I pinball around the deep pools. Do I lower my pack over the six-foot drop into sand and jump? Or de-boot and wade across? I loop my laces through a carabiner on my pack, slip into flip flops and roll my pants to mid-thigh. My pants still get wet, but I make it, and my peacock feathers puff.

The path narrows and I greet Likya's waymarks with good mornings and love taps. After two hours, I savour my last orange, Teoman's gift, and look into the canyon from 500 metres above. How can we possibly think we're in control? All this nature, all this vastness, working together? We are specks on Earth, and we damage it. It? Us. Everything connects.

Up until a few days ago, Likya plants pricked and scraped, but now, soft Likya plants snuggle my lower calves and skinny stems puff out to velvet leaves that caress my arms. But Helicopter Bug still annoys, performing military drills at my eye level—right, left, down, up. Birds sing like classical pianists, others like reversing dump trucks, both melodic.

Body, good. Feet, good. Trail, good. Attitude of gratitude. All is well.

My mind loosens further and drifts back. I didn't write about it. I've written long journal entries, detail after detail, every day. But not last night. *Made it to the canyon and camped.* Why only that? Nothing about Teoman? Why didn't I write about it? What am I hiding from myself? I didn't do anything wrong. Did I?

No, you didn't.

If something had happened—"But it wouldn't have been my fucking fault!"

You're right. And it wasn't then either.

What?

A blurry image. Two more, three more, like a filmstrip with 30 years of grime. I walk it into clarity. A party upstairs. A basement. A couch. Kisses. Laughter. He was older, sixteen, seventeen? Rough hands explored. Full body pushed down. "No." Squirms underneath. "No. No!" Lips silenced, by lips. Arms forced flat. Please, no. Shorts yanked aside. Fingers forced in. Stillness.

It was only fingers, so not a real sexual assault, and besides, we had been kissing, my fourteen-year-old self had thought. So I didn't tell anyone, ever. I wasn't ready. I'm still not.

I walk on.

In the early afternoon, the forest shoots me out onto an unmarked dirt road. Which way? Right? I follow the river, and then I find a low suspension bridge and shady picnic tables. I'm here already? Hundreds of teenagers swarm, okay, maybe 24. But within minutes, the kids finish eating and the women behind the outdoor counter smile despite being slammed with stacks of dirty dishes. I sip water in the shade until they get a handle on the rush, and in the meantime, I unfold my final laminated map.

It's early still, if I can get food to go and fill up my water, do I start the final section? Really?

The young worker offers hamburgers, grilled fish and chicken.

"Um, vegetarian?"

"We can do a salad?"

"Perfect, teşekkür ederim, and I'm hiking the Likya Yolu. Do you have something I can take?"

The older man at the outdoor grill disappears into a little wood cabin and returns holding a hunk of bread.

"Cheese, tomatoes, peppers?"

"Evet, great!"

After my salad, the young worker hands me cheese sandwiches with whole tomatoes and peppers.

"You have these, in Canada?"

"Red peppers? Evet."

"They are good for you, help with cancer."

"Very good for you. I'm so happy for this, thank you."

"Good to see happy people, you are very happy, the world is so—" and draws a frown on his face.

"You should've seen me three days ago."

"Well, you'll like the rest, it's like a rainforest, and there's good camping in a few hours."

"Thank you for everything, almost done."

And within minutes, a wooden sign with red electrical wire twisted into letters—*Hisarçandir 18km*. Here we go.

An hour in, Likya guides me and rock cairns assist, and I build even more rock towers to add to the directions. Two hours in, silence. No bugs, no birds, no wind, no cars, nothing but my breath. Three hours in, a sizeable mossy area opens up. Wait, is this that area on the map, the one near a stream with a trickle of water? Beyond this, dense trees surround a cozy mossy section, and I drop my pack.

Now in my camp clothes and flip flops, I investigate in the dusk, bushwhack through the brush and leapfrog across smooth stones, the remnants of a tiny dry river bed. Shhh, wait, is that it? Drip. Drip. Drip. Yes! I backtrack, gather clothes and supplies and return to the source. First, I filter water and fill my water pack. Then a few steps down-trickle, in a pool the size of a farm sink, I strip and delight in a stand up bath, just me and Mother Nature. As I air dry, I wash my hiking clothes before returning to camp.

By 6 o'clock, I recline in my chair and munch a handful of leftover gözleme as my toes squish moss. One sandwich for tomorrow and the other sandwich the following day. And then... I'm done. Done?

I write for two hours but the pen dawdles. It seems I want to slow the speed of everything—writing, hiking, bathing, eating—and I pause yet again to look up. Will I keep this new practice of gazing into the sky?

DAY 28

(Near) Hisarçandir to (Almost) Hisarçandir

E ACH TIME I RAISE MY HEAD, Likya greets me and lures me up the steady incline, and I return thanks with GoodMorningGünaydinMerhabas. An abundance of rock cairns connect the waymarks and I build dozens more. It's shady, yet I sweat. It's silent, except the crunch-squish underfoot, from needles fallen from pine trees that end at a sharp line, only a rock face leading to the top, and—Hole Mountain! A rough, chunky hole-in-the-rock that my book describes as big as a bus. A good reminder to look up more.

As the sun lifts over the ridge, the lyrics of "You Are My Sunshine" float beside me. Papa's song.

"You are my sunsh—"

"My only sunsh—"

In the solitude, tears flow easy and my handkerchief soaks. Papa, his crib board, and me, finally absorbing how to play the game. And Nana, oh Nana. And Grandma, Grandma's vegetable soup! Stringy onions clinging to the wooden spoon as she stirred the aluminum WearEver pot, homemade bread slices dangling over plate edges. Grandma's soup spoon, and Grandpa, and Grandpa's spoons! I thought playing the spoons back-to-back was your own musical invention, Grandpa, until I saw another Grandpa playing the spoons at a French cultural festival. You're French. I am French. Grandpa, and dad. Dad. What a year of transition for you. "Here Comes the Sun" floats in and I sing along. I love playing all your original Beatles albums, Dad. Your signature penned in the corners, listening to the crackles as they play on my 1983 Fisher turntable. The Beatles make me feel, what? Connected. To family. Dad, my sister, and mom. Mom. It's been eight years; she would've been so excited for me to hike here. And to friends, best friends who gathered with me at the ocean, to honour a dog after I said my final goodbye.

Bumblebees visit gangly sunflowers as the soft leaves stroke my skin. Why does that feel so tender, so loving?

"And, I saaay, it's alllright."

Just before 10 o'clock, logs around a stone fire pit beg me to rest. A handful of peanuts and four pieces of cheese? I have no idea how I can expend so much energy, yet a small breakfast can satisfy. I'm going to take lots of ten minute breaks today, even five minutes every hour cools and energizes me. Why don't I do that when I work?

The path widens and blends into an open mountainside. Pine trees thin, and clouds and mist blend to fill in the spaces. Visibility shrinks to 30 feet. For the first time on the trail, goosebumps replace sweat, and I'm not clear if it's because of the temperature drop or The Fog. Airline passengers at 36,000 feet give brief, but welcome, companionship.

Trees blackened by fire or lightning stand despite adversity, others succumb. I barrel roll over the fallen logs, arms and legs suspending for a moment in a loose hug. One ancient tree orders a drop and crawl manoeuvre and I squish the last tomato in my pack when I squeeze underneath.

Once back into the trees for switchbacks, every third step, my heart and lungs recalibrate, as my face, neck and arms drench with sweat and mist. Swist? Smeat? I continue to build rock cairns and after one impressive stack, a ladybug crowns it.

At noon, a flat area the size of a six-person tent juts with monster-size rock slabs that I scramble around and in-between. And then, the trail drops. Wait. Down? Was that the top? Already?

A half hour later, a dribble of water calls me over, and I gorge, filling my water pack and extra water bottle too.

The map shows I'm almost done, and close to the road. I feel, weird. What is this feeling? I still say merhaba and I love you to all the waymarks, but I don't know this new feeling. Glum? Sad? No, that's not it.

I don't know how far to go. Oh how I want *tuz*—salt—on potato chips and French fries. But I don't want to go to Antalya today. I want to camp one more night, one more night of quiet reflection. I'm not ready for Antalya. I know that.

Damn, it's the road.

"Merhaba," says a man.

"Merhaba," I say and join the group picnic in the woods.

"You are alone?"

"Yes, I started in Ovacik."

"You are by yourself?" he asks again.

"Evet."

"How many kilometres?"

"Maybe 450?"

"Whew!" and he translates for the others who smile.

"Okay, almost done, güle güle."

A wide dirt road winds down the hill, the only one to Hisarçandir. So it's time for tunes, and Shuffle selects my favourites: Matchbox 20's "How Far We've Come," Coldplay's

"Don't Panic," KT Tunstall's "Suddenly I See" and The Eels' "Novocaine for Your Soul" and on and on. But I'm feeling a bit off. I know it's because I'm finishing. I thought I'd be excited, relieved to be done. Maybe tomorrow? I don't know. My pace slows but not because of tender soles. The road is bulldozed hard-pack dirt, has Likya been bulldozed too? Earlier, there was a yellow sign—*Hisarçandir 8kms*—but I haven't seen a waymark since. For 28 days Likya has guided me, and these last days, I've said hello to every single one—every one. Today, I blew kisses. Now, gone. I didn't even say goodbye.

"Likya, you're here."

And below the red and white paint, a tortoise truckin' along.

I follow him from 20 feet back so I can watch him, but I eventually catch up.

"Hi tortoise." I wave. He doesn't.

The road winds through the expansive valley for what seems longer than eight kilometres, and I appreciate the time warp. Where can I camp for my last night? I scan the steep sides of the bulldozed cliffs and look for any access off the road. There. A scramble up the loose rocks lands me in the pine trees, and I bushwhack deeper until I'm hidden from the road. I drop my pack and complete my routine for the last time.

Goat bells and the call to prayer ring up the valley. Oh Turkey, you've been good to me. A shepherd yells, so okay, that means no dogs, no Kangals. The clouds and mist erase the valley view as I shiver in all my clothes and jacket, so I retreat inside. With no more food, I can't camp again. Is Hisarçandir big enough for a pansiyon? I curl into my down sleeping bag but with no need for an alarm, my Likya routine ends.

DAY 29

(Almost) Hisarçandir to Hisarçandir

I SLIP INTO FLIP FLOPS, DIVE feet first through the tent vestibule and surface into the sightlines of a Turkish Kangal. Twenty feet away. Silent. His collar of two-inch metal spikes—protection against predators—confirms his dedication and work ethic.

"Uh, merhaba, puppy," I whisper.

The quiet confident ones scare me. At 19 and on a camp-out with friends, I walked back from the outhouse and met a muscular hound who tiptoed to within inches. At a stand-off, I turned sideways, eyes averted. He lunged anyways. No bark, only calculated execution of teeth. The scar on my left cheek no longer shows, but I still feel it.

"Merhaba, puppy," I whisper and squat. "Just have to pee, don't take offence."

As I turn back around, 20 feet on the other side of my tent? Another Kangal.

"Shit."

My heart leaps into nylon safety, and my body tumbles on top. With the door open, I whisper sweet nothings to Spike, as I fumble with my things and ignore the packing protocol. Dogs bark in the village, but Spike doesn't flinch. One ear flicks when a car drives by, but his eyes target me. Have they stalked me all night?

"Go home, puppy." Nothing.

What if I wait them out? Ooo, raindrops, maybe now they'll take off? Spike looks up, then locks back on me: *I've got all day.*

Maybes Spike's got spikes because he's actually a soft and cuddly Kangal? Hey boo-boo kitty! How about a steak? Um, well, peanuts? Your buddy can eat too.

I contort to stuff my pack with everything but the tent. It's time. I stand up outside and haul it out. Spike holds his ground. The smaller, fuzzier, younger one too. Learning to stalk? I reach back inside for my rolled sleeping pad and turn, and—Spike's gone. I whip around—the fuzzy one's gone too. I scan the mountain slope. Gone.

My backpack is light, water pack half-full, no food. One pole thuds, the other now a metallic click, the rubber cap worn out. How is it the clicking one always ends up in my left hand? I pause at the yellow and black Likya sign that appears—*Hisarçandir 2 kms.* Two kilometres. My footsteps slow into walking meditation. Left. Right. Why did I rush before? I'm feeling weird again. Sadness? No. What is this feeling? I still look for Likya, and then—

"Lik—" my voice cracks as my gut crunches.

"Likya Yo—"

Behind sunglasses, my handkerchief dabs at my wet eyes.

"Likya Yolu."

I stand in front of the waymark painted on the rock wall. The signs. The guidance. My fingers trace the red and white paint.

"Teşekkür ederim, Likya Yolu, teşekkür ederim."

A lone truck slows as the driver rolls down his window.

"It was good? The Likya?" asks the passenger.

"Evet," I say as my sunglasses fog up. "It was good."

My thoughts drift back to the dogs. Really? Right up to my last day? Stalking me all night and then vanishing when I'm ready to go? I stop.

Wolves. Bears. Jackals. Guardians of the night—

My hands clasp over my heart as I inhale deep. You weren't protecting your sheep. You were protecting *me*. My exhale releases love for the Kangals, all the hard-working, dedicated Kangals. Teşekkür ederim.

Slow. No music. I want to hear the birds, the dogs, my footsteps, the water flowing along a channel off to the right of the road, the slosh in my almost empty hydration pack. As the sun rises behind me, my shadow stretches in front—hiker girl—my sleeping pad extends past my hips, the ripped flaps from the jagged rocks en route to Kaş. The village's red roofs get bigger in-between the pine trees. Baa-aa-aa. Roosters. A mosque tower. I'm almost here. And Likya is here too.

"Likya Yolu, mer-ha-ba!"

"Likya Yolu, gün-ay-din."

"Likya Yolu, güle güle."

Goodbye.

Will hikers crowd the end? Will they high five me? Or will I be alone? I don't know which I want more. Wait, I haven't seen any hikers in three days, what makes me think there might be a crowd?

The dirt road ends at asphalt. Left or right?

"Merhaba," says a woman sweeping amongst chickens.

"Merhaba. Likya? Cami?" I ask and sweep my left arm wide and then the right.

She does the same. Okay, either way. Which way will you go, Michelle? I wind downhill and pass more houses with chickens. Parked FIAT 124s make the narrow street narrower. I'm on the last turn, and the mosque tower comes up too fast. Heel-toe, heel-toe. I can't walk any slower. Are those the Likya boards? A quiet highway crosses ahead marking the end of my road.

My breath holds. My feet hold. And my tears hold. Twenty feet. Ten feet. And then, I'm here. I said goodbye to Likya back up the hill, and now, it's simply over. I don't jump for joy, I don't collapse, I just stand under the blue mosque tower and feel the moment with the two signs, one a start—*509kms*—and the other an end—*0 kms*.

And I know this emotion now. I know what I'm feeling. It's not sadness, it's not happiness. It's more neutral.

That blankness?

It's peace. I'm at peace.

I drop my pack and pose it against the signs for the photo op. Now what? It's only 9 o'clock in the morning. Antalya's 25 kilometres away. Dolmuş? Where do I catch it? When? I could walk?

A Peugeot coasts towards me.

"*Taksi*? Antalya?" asks the driver.

"Dolmuş?"

"At eight in the morning or eight at night."

I scan the barely legible *taksi* on the door and faded Turkey Tourism logo on the back but allow him to continue his impersonation.

"One hundred lira," he says

"Ah, no, I'll walk."

"Okay, 80 lira."

"Sixty lira to Argos Hotel in Kaleiçi."

"Okay, 60 lira," he says as he stuffs my pack through the back door.

He smiles in the rear view mirror as I pat for a seatbelt, but with none, I'm free to twist back to Likya. Our gaze lingers until I roll through the stop sign and turn right towards home.

That's my girl.

ACKNOWLEDGEMENTS

Thank you to my friends and family, especially Heather, Kate, Robyn and Sarah, who offered support by regularly checking in and asking, "how's the book coming along?"

Thank you to my editor, Kathy Garland, for her guidance and suggestions that helped make this a better book.

Many thanks to Altuğ Şenel, co-creator of the lycianway.org and likyayolu.org websites and administrator of the Lycian Way Facebook group, for his help in answering my many questions by email, both before the hike and after.

And a huge thank-you to Semih Fisekci, a local Gabriola artist who is originally from Turkey and who spent many hours with me discussing Turkish customs and the language to ensure accuracy in this book. Any errors in these pages are mine alone.

I would like to express my gratitude to the many people on my Facebook author page, especially Eileen, Fran, Renee and Theresa, who commented with words of encouragement and excitement as I shared the preparation for the hike and the journey of writing this book. The true value of your words was, and is, immense and I thank you.

And finally, I'd like to thank everyone who I crossed paths with in the mountain villages, the coastal towns and along the trail. Each person was exactly who I was meant, and needed, to meet.

Teşekkür ederim.

WORKS CITED

Clow, Kate. *The Lycian Way: Turkey's First Long Distance Walking Route* (3rd ed.). Upcountry (Turkey) Ltd, 2009. Print.

Gray, David. "Transformation." *Draw the Line.* Downtown/Mercer Street Records, 2009. MP3.

O'Connor, Sinéad. "Old Lady." By Sinéad O'Connor and Marco Pirroni. *How About I Be Me (And You Be You)?* One Little Indian/Relativity, 2012. MP3.

Train. "Blind." *Train.* Aware Records. 1998, MP3.

Train. "Drops of Jupiter." *Drops of Jupiter.* Columbia/Sony BMG, 2001. MP3.

Train. "Eggplant." *Train.* Aware Records, 1998. MP3.

Train. "For Me, It's You." *For Me, It's You.* Columbia, 2006. MP3.

Train. "I'm About to Come Alive." *Train.* Aware Records, 1998. MP3.

Train. "It's About You." *Drops of Jupiter.* Columbia/Sony BMG, 2001. MP3.

Train. "I Wish You Would." *Drops of Jupiter*. Columbia/Sony BMG, 2001. MP3.

Train. "Mississippi." *Drops of Jupiter*. Columbia/Sony BMG, 2001. MP3.

Train. "Respect." *Drops of Jupiter*. Columbia/Sony BMG, 2001. MP3.

Train. "Something More." *Drops of Jupiter*. Columbia/Sony BMG, 2001. MP3.

TRADEMARKS

As listed below, registered and unregistered trademarks are used in this book and are used without permission. Use of the trademark is not authorized by, associated with or sponsored by the trademark owner.

Coke is a trademark of The Coca-Cola Company.

COPS is a trademark of Langley Productions, Inc.

DeFeet and Woolie Boolie are trademarks of DeFeet International.

Efes is a trademark of Anadolu Efes

FIAT is a trademark of FIAT Group Marketing & Corporate Communication S.p.A.

Godzilla is a trademark of Toho Co. Ltd.

Google and Google Translate are trademarks of Google Inc.

Jaws is a trademark of Universal City Studios LLC.

Minnie Mouse is a trademark of Disney Enterprises, Inc.

MSR Hubba NX is a trademark of Cascade Designs, Inc.

Peugeot is a trademark of Peugeot SA.

SkyTrain is a trademark of South Coast British Columbia Transportation Authority ("TransLink").

Swiss Army Knife is a trademark of Victorinox AG.

Tekel 2001 is a trademark of Tekel/British American Tobacco.

Therm-a-Rest is a trademark of Cascade Designs, Inc.

Titanic Belfast is a trademark of Titanic Belfast Limited.

Vibram is trademark of Vibram S.p.A.

WearEver is a trademark of WearEver.

Weeble is a trademark of Hasbro, Inc.

WhatsApp is a trademark of WhatsApp Inc.

A NOTE FROM THE AUTHOR

Merhaba!

Thank you so much for reading *Breaking the Fourth Wall: An Uncertain Journey on Turkey's Lycian Way*. If you enjoyed it, please take a moment to leave a review on Goodreads or your favourite online retailer such as Amazon.

I welcome all contact from readers. On my website, you can email me, sign up for my email newsletter to be notified of new book releases and find links to connect with me on social media.

Also on my website, are photos, song playlists and resources to accompany this book.

www.michellesevigny.com

— Michelle Sevigny

ABOUT THE AUTHOR

Michelle Sevigny is an entrepreneur, writer, dog lover and wannabe sailor. She has a degree in communications and is the author of *Dogsafe: Everything Your Dog Wants You to Know in an Emergency*. She lives and writes in a tiny cabin on Gabriola Island, on the west coast of Canada. www.michellesevigny.com

Made in the USA
Monee, IL
23 June 2020